CHINESE NEW YEAR COLORING BOOK

THIS BOOK BELONGS TO:

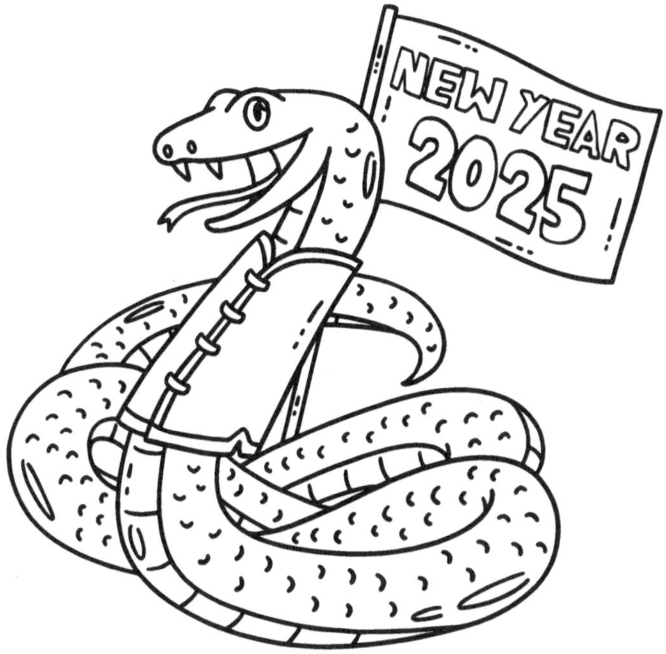

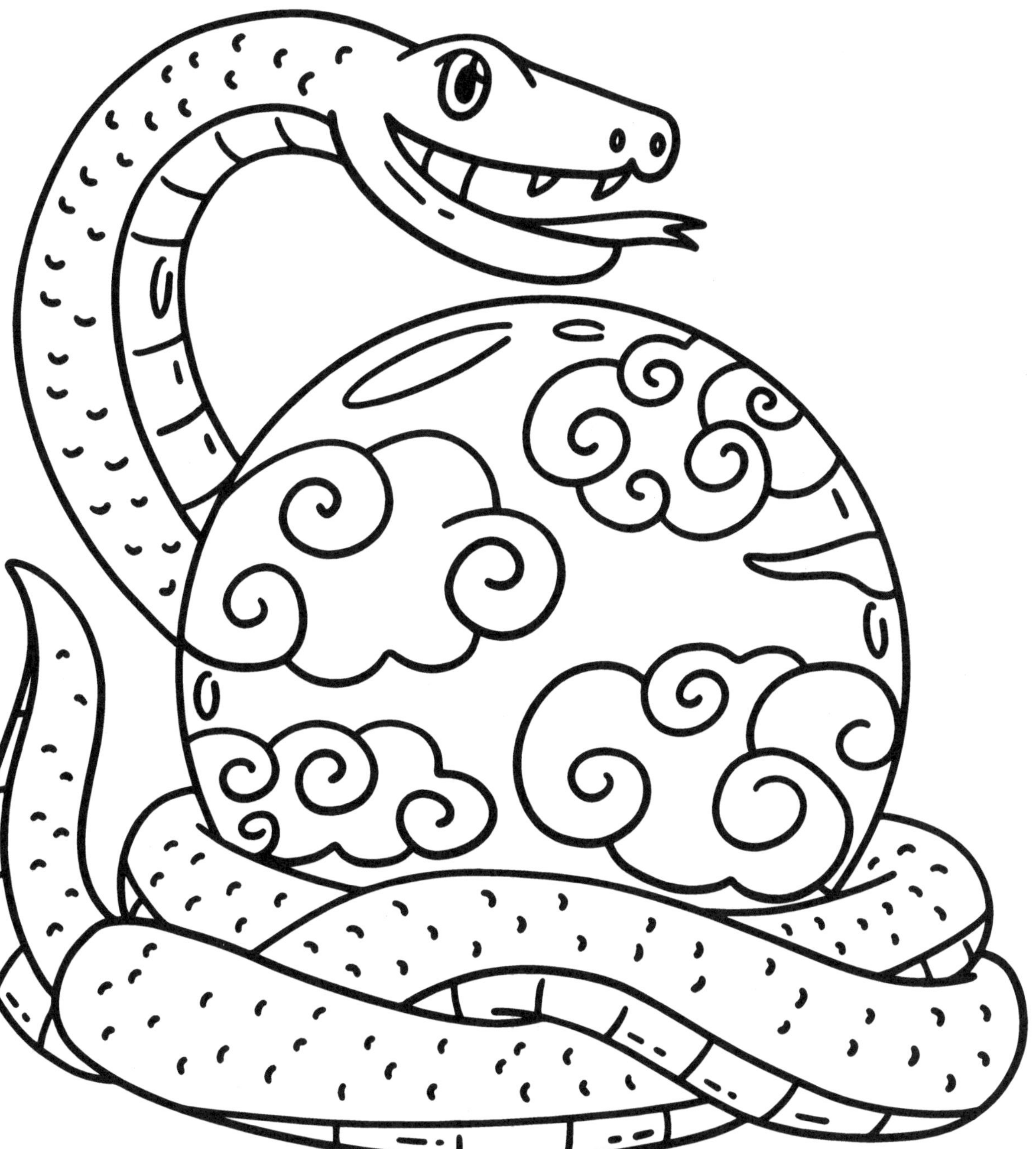

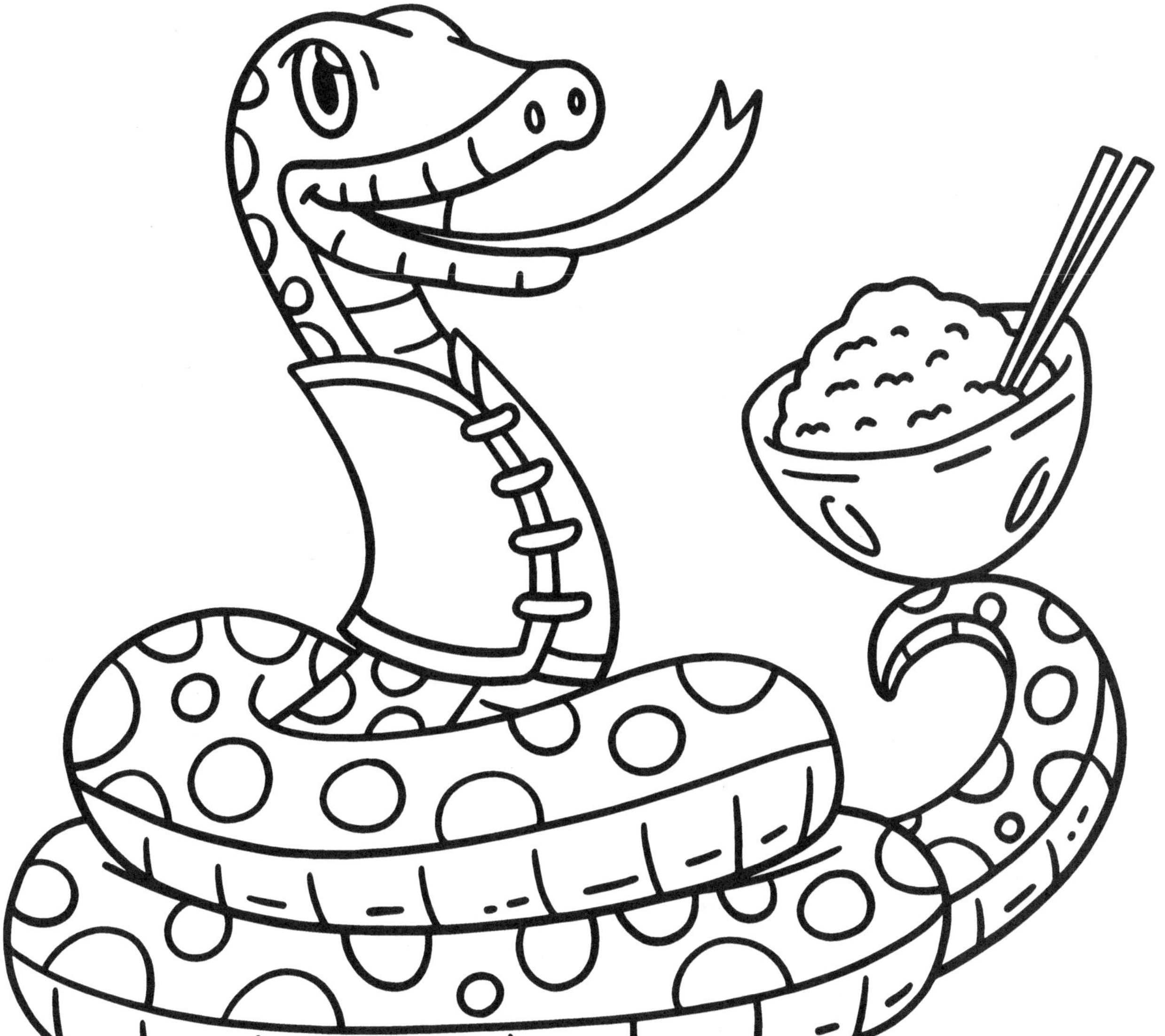

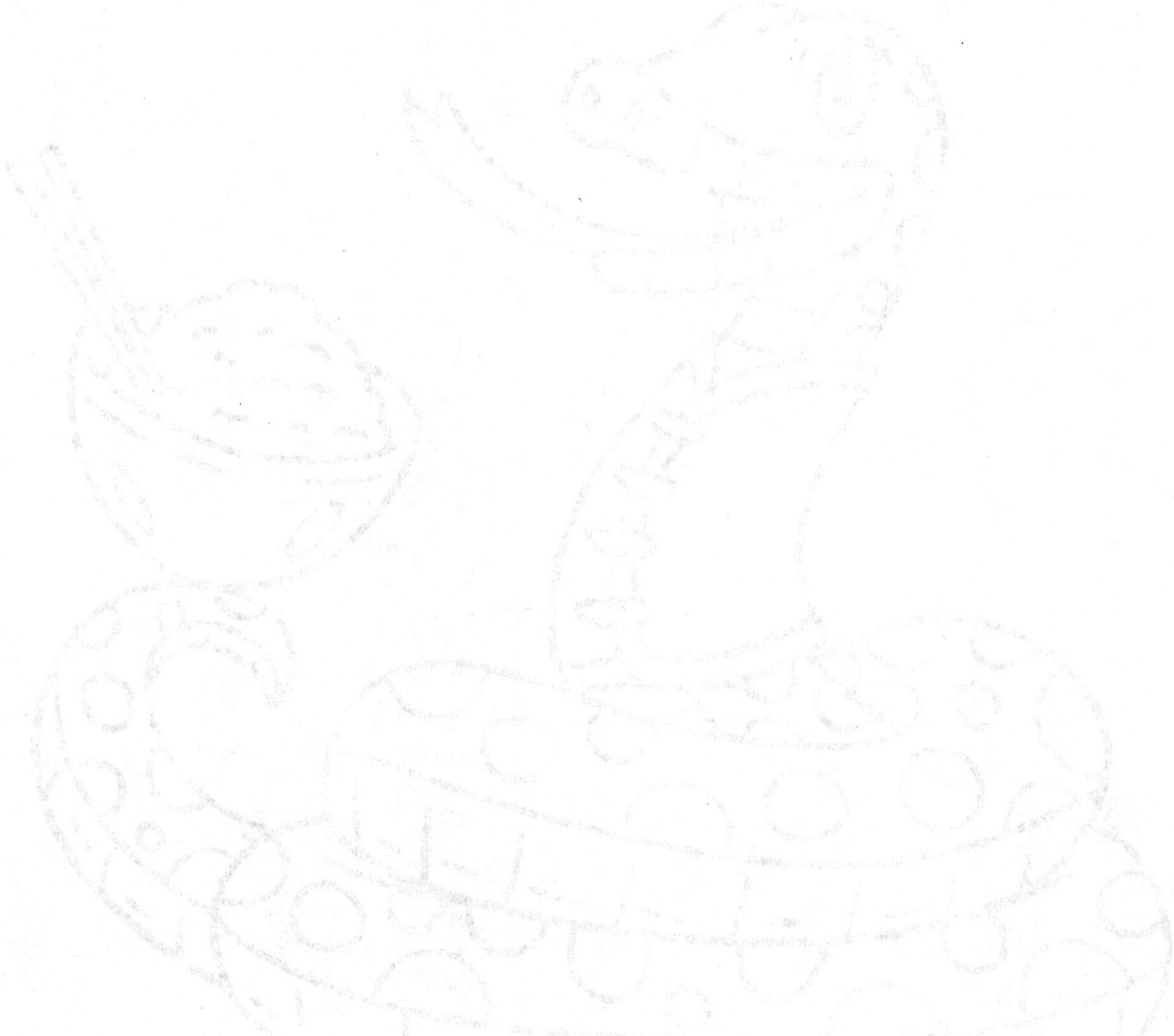

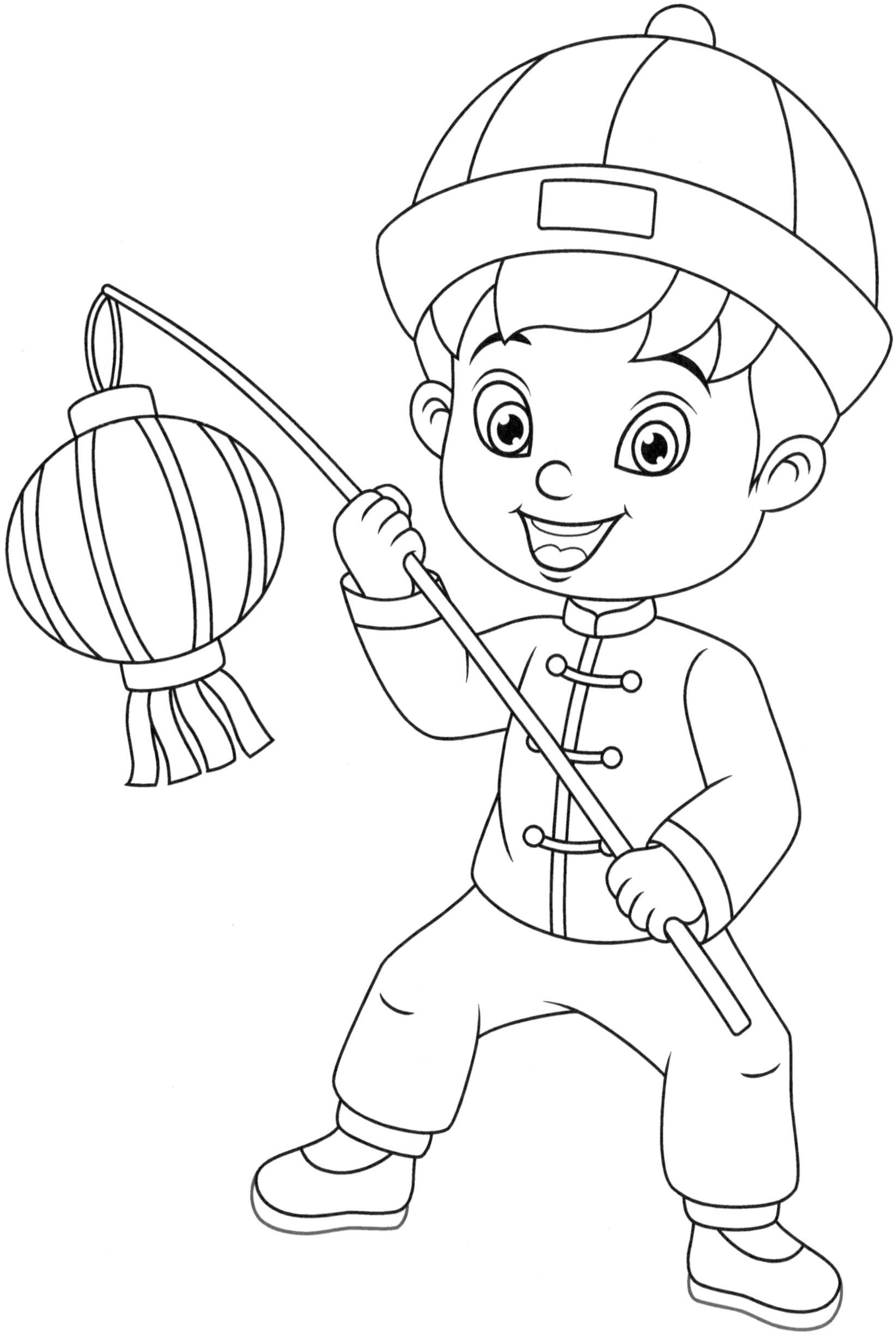

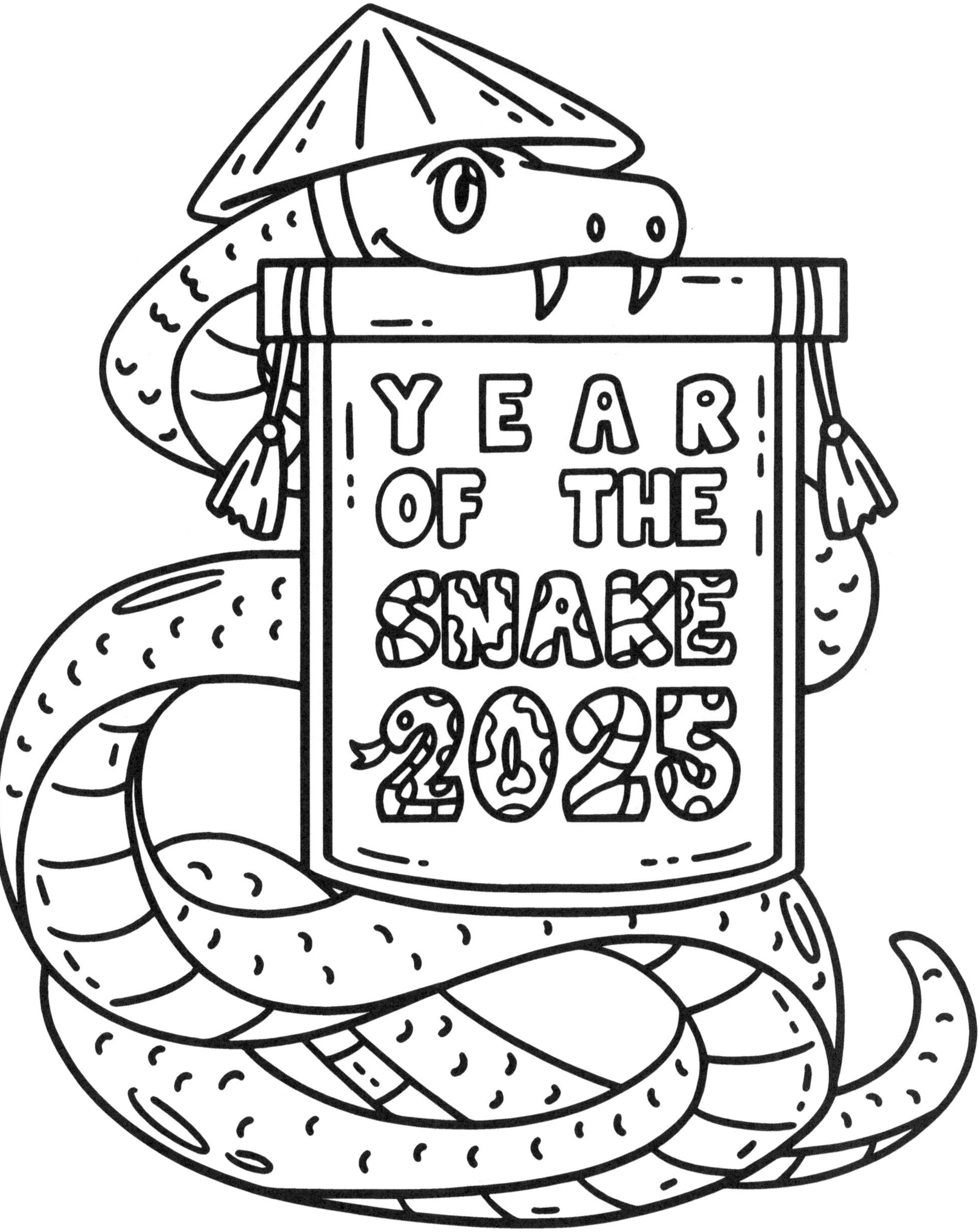
YEAR
OF THE
SNAKE
2025

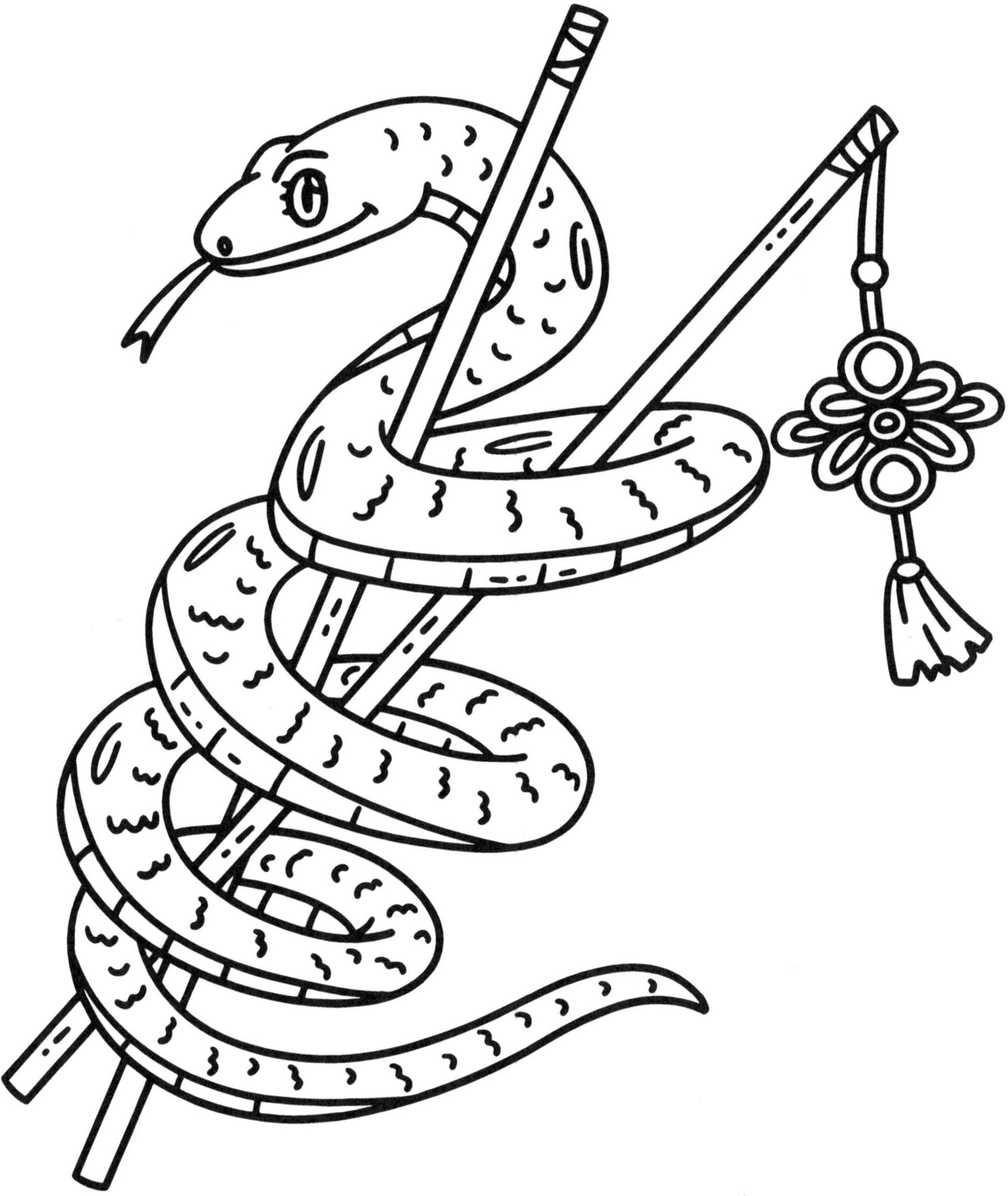

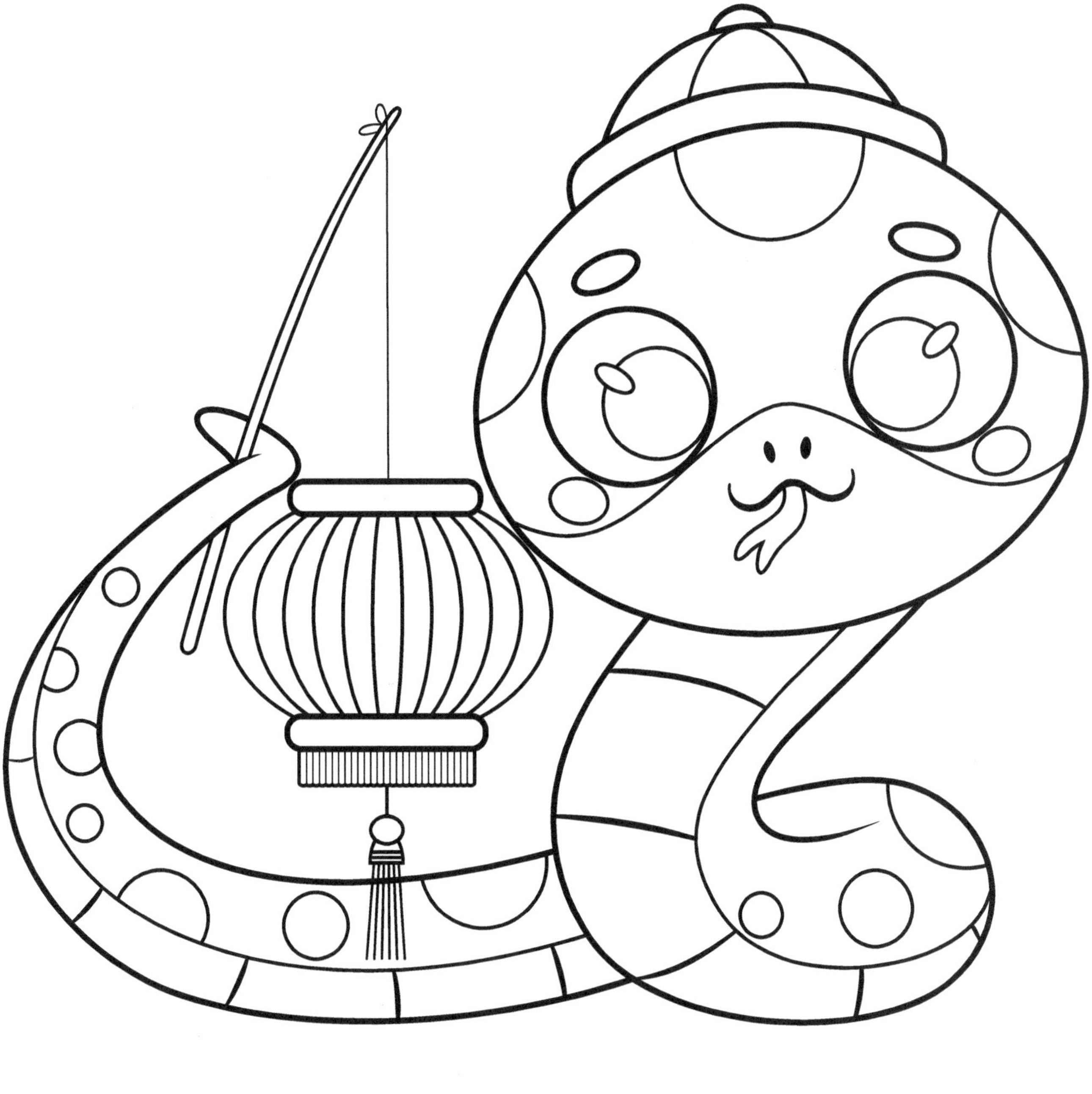

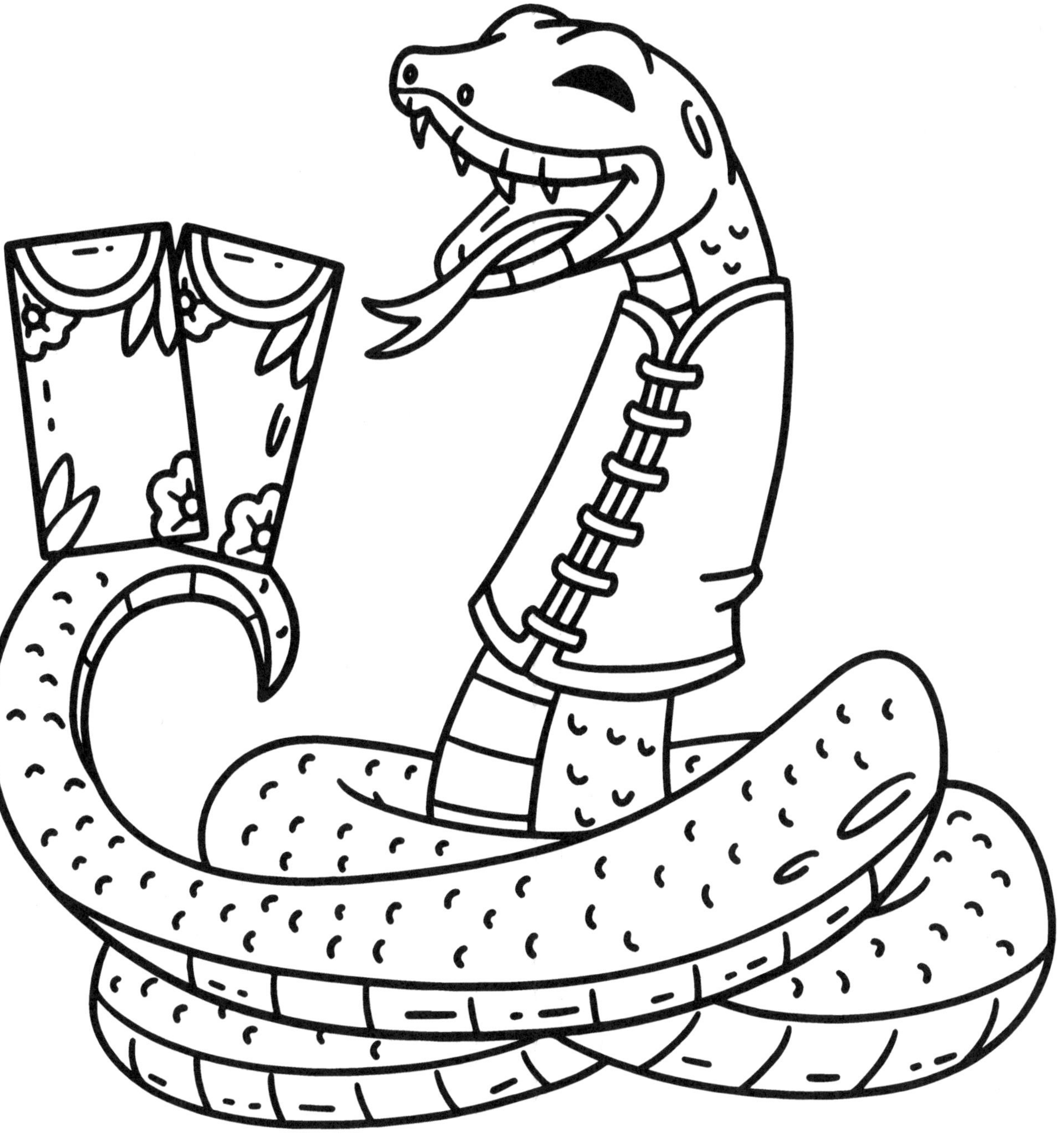

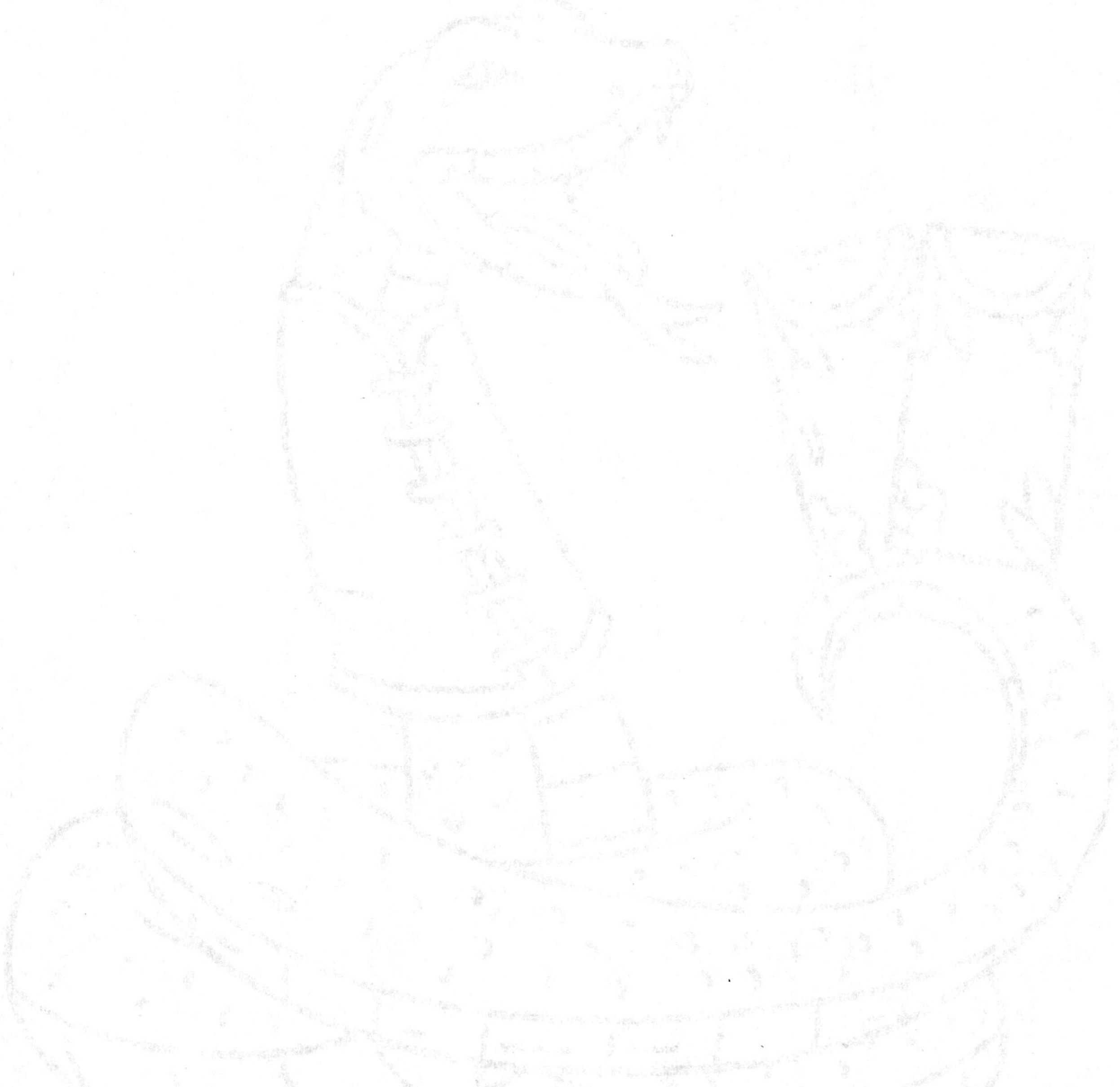

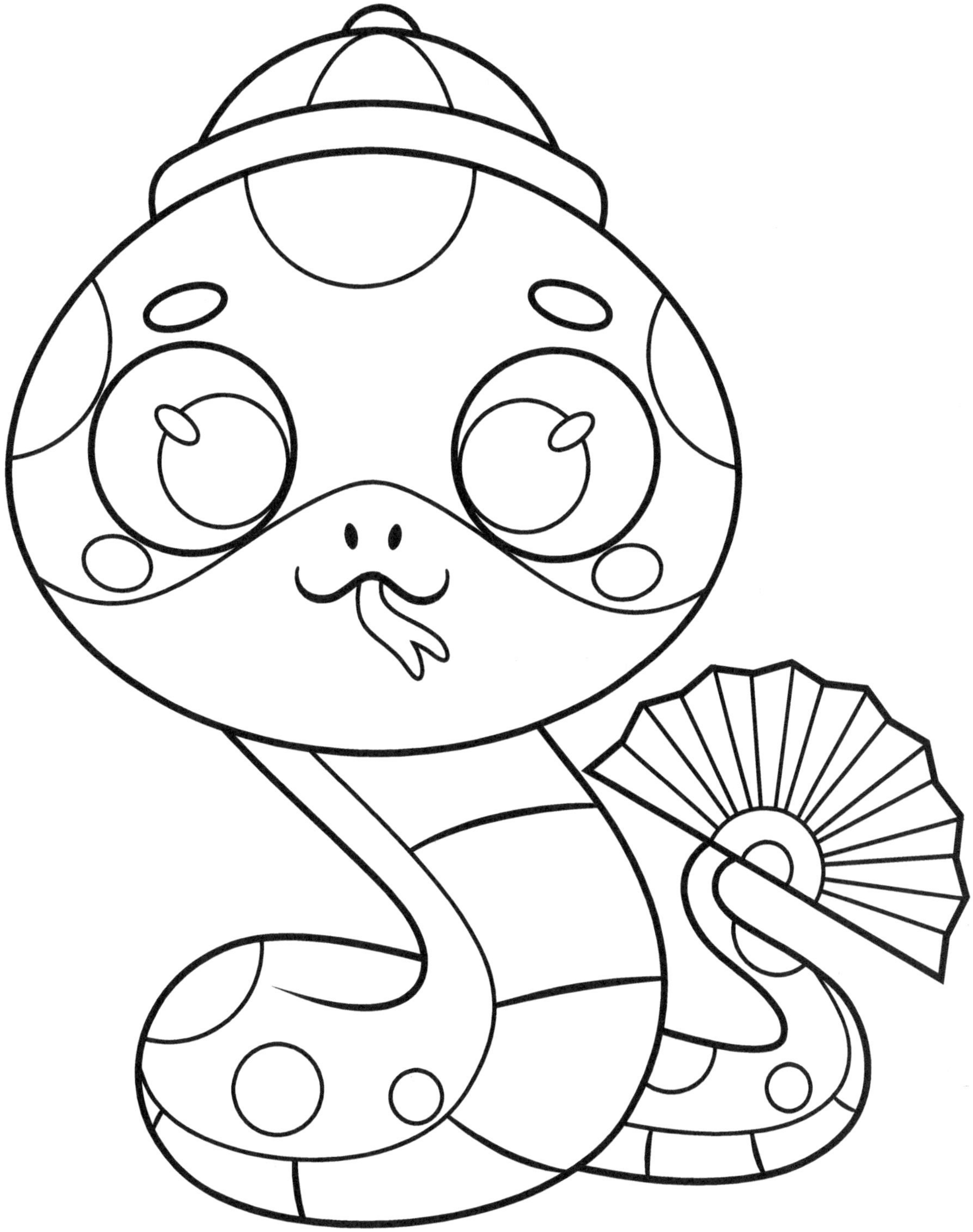

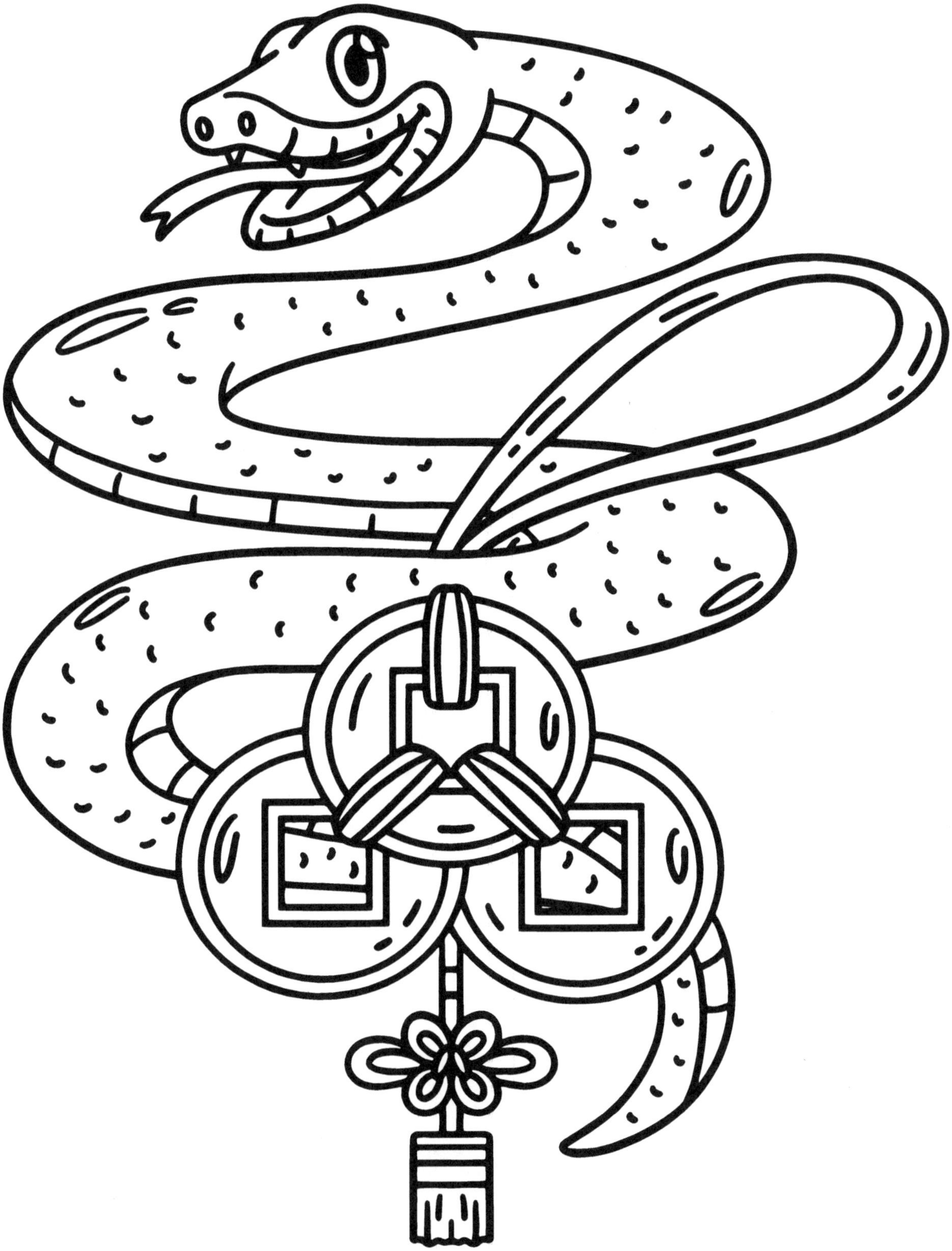

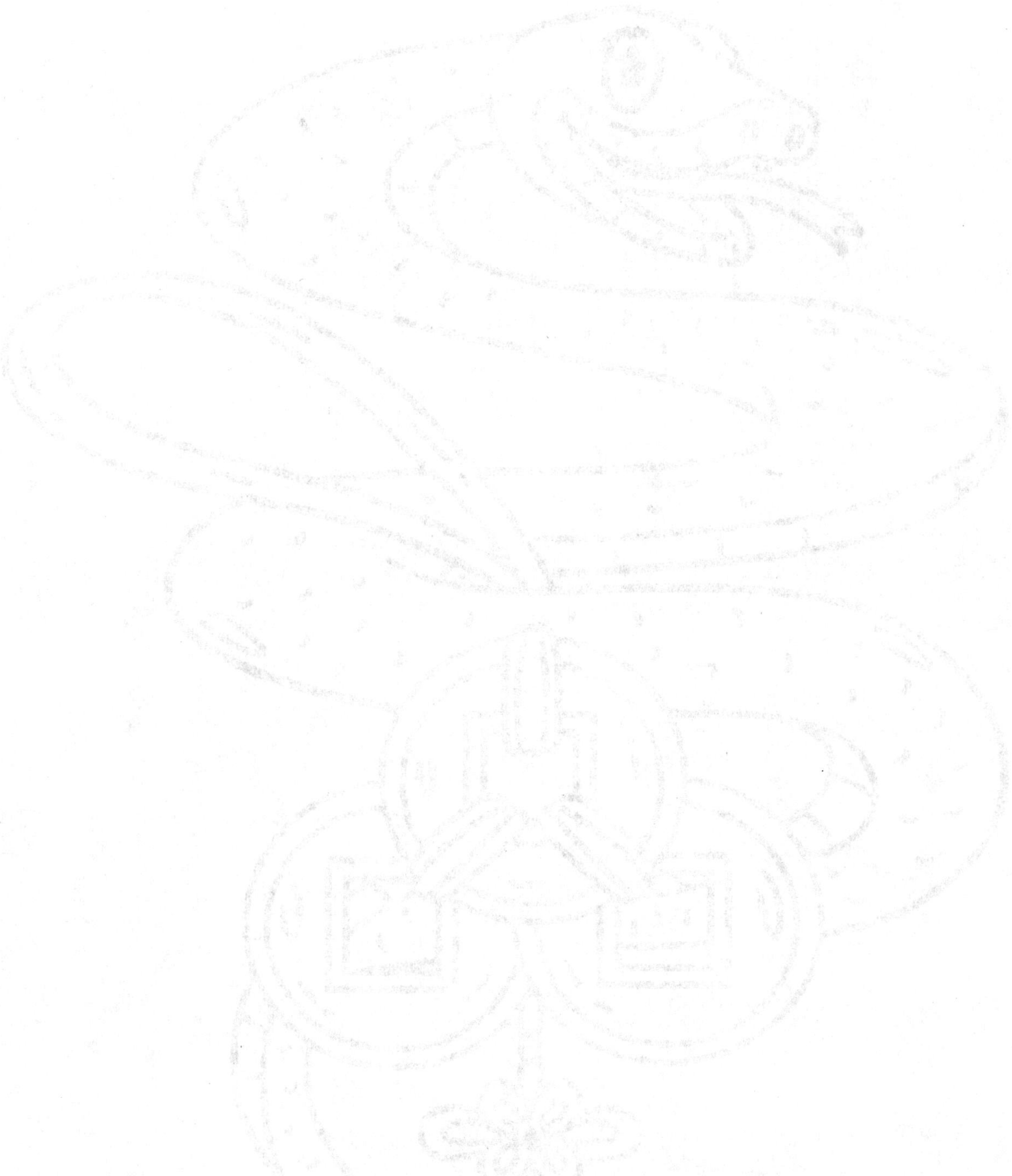

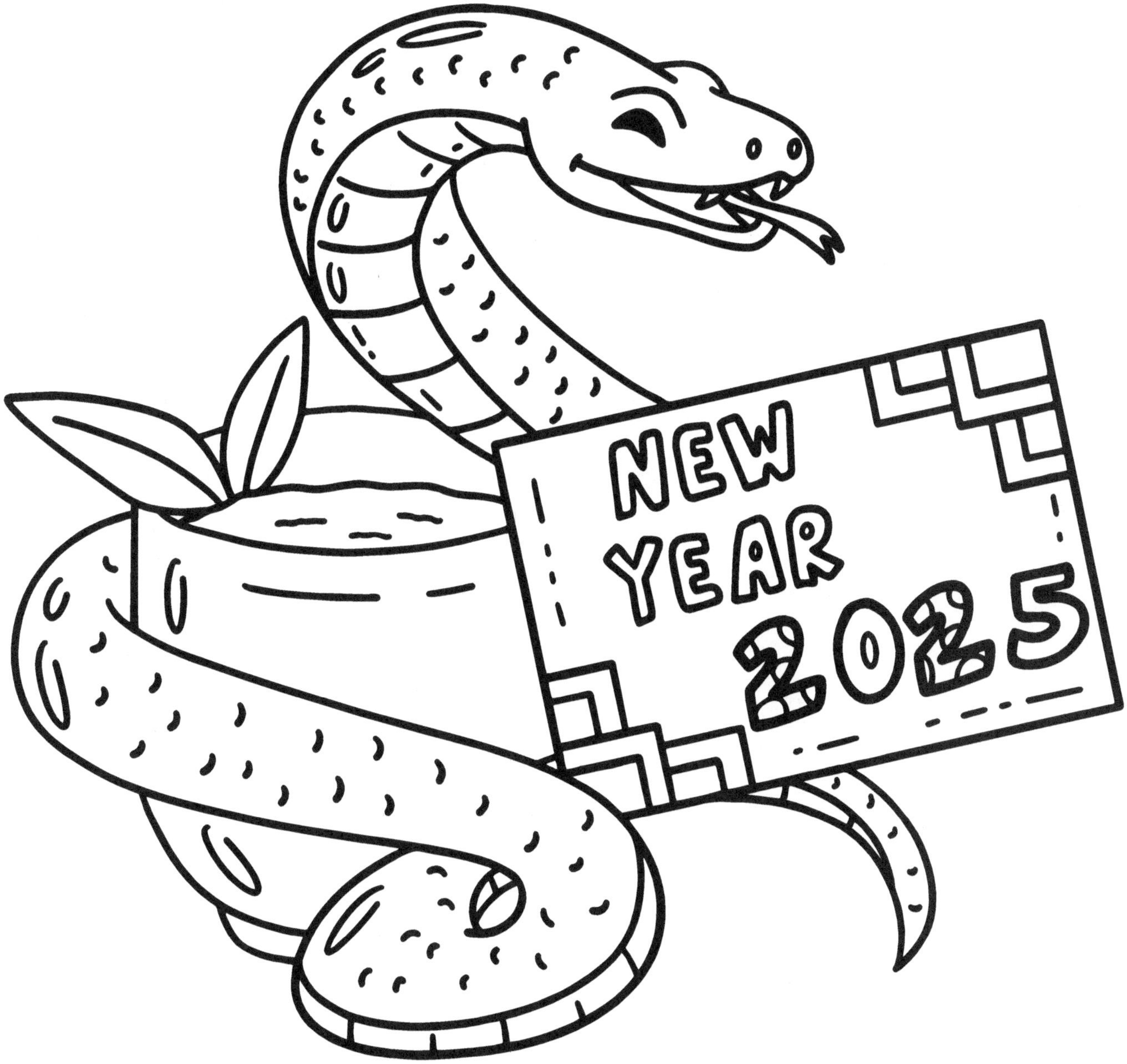
NEW
YEAR
2025

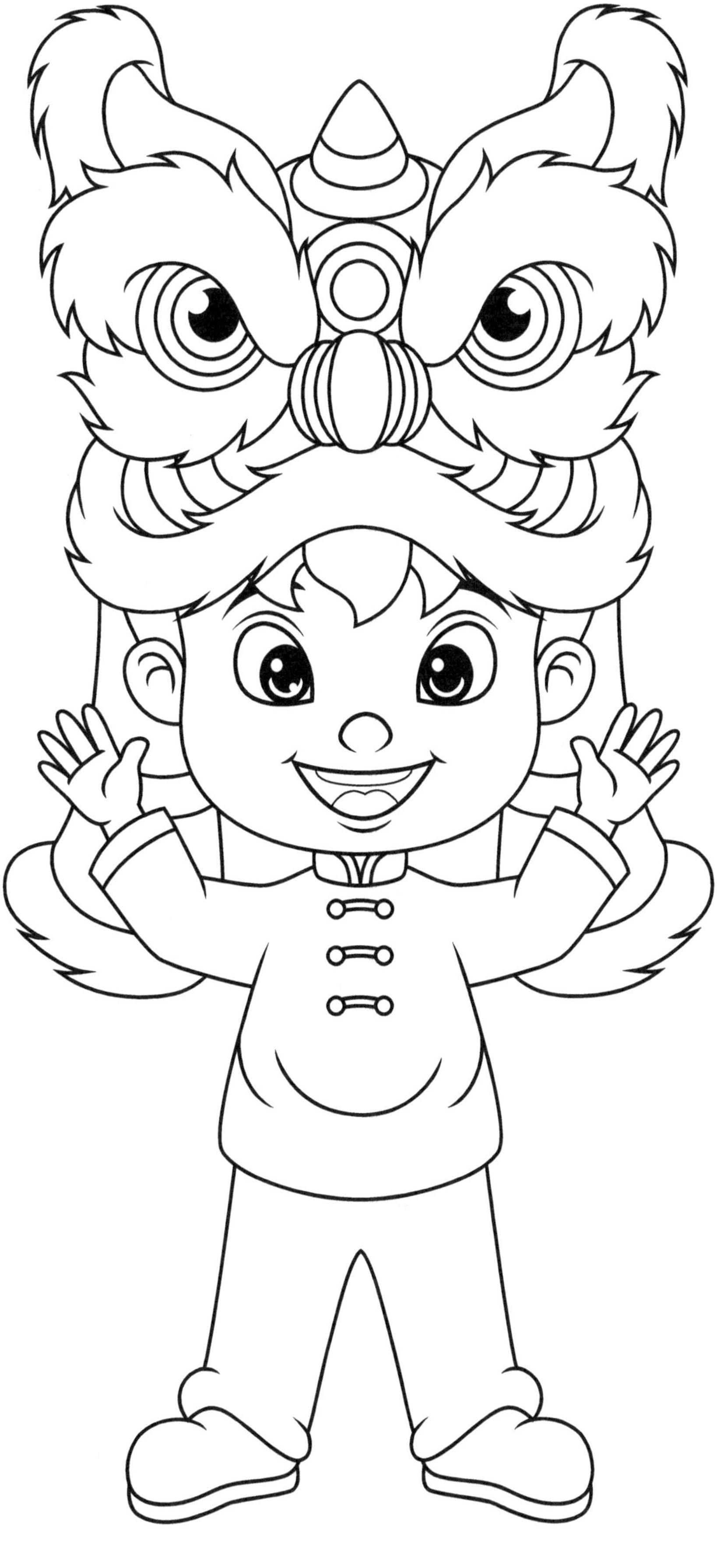

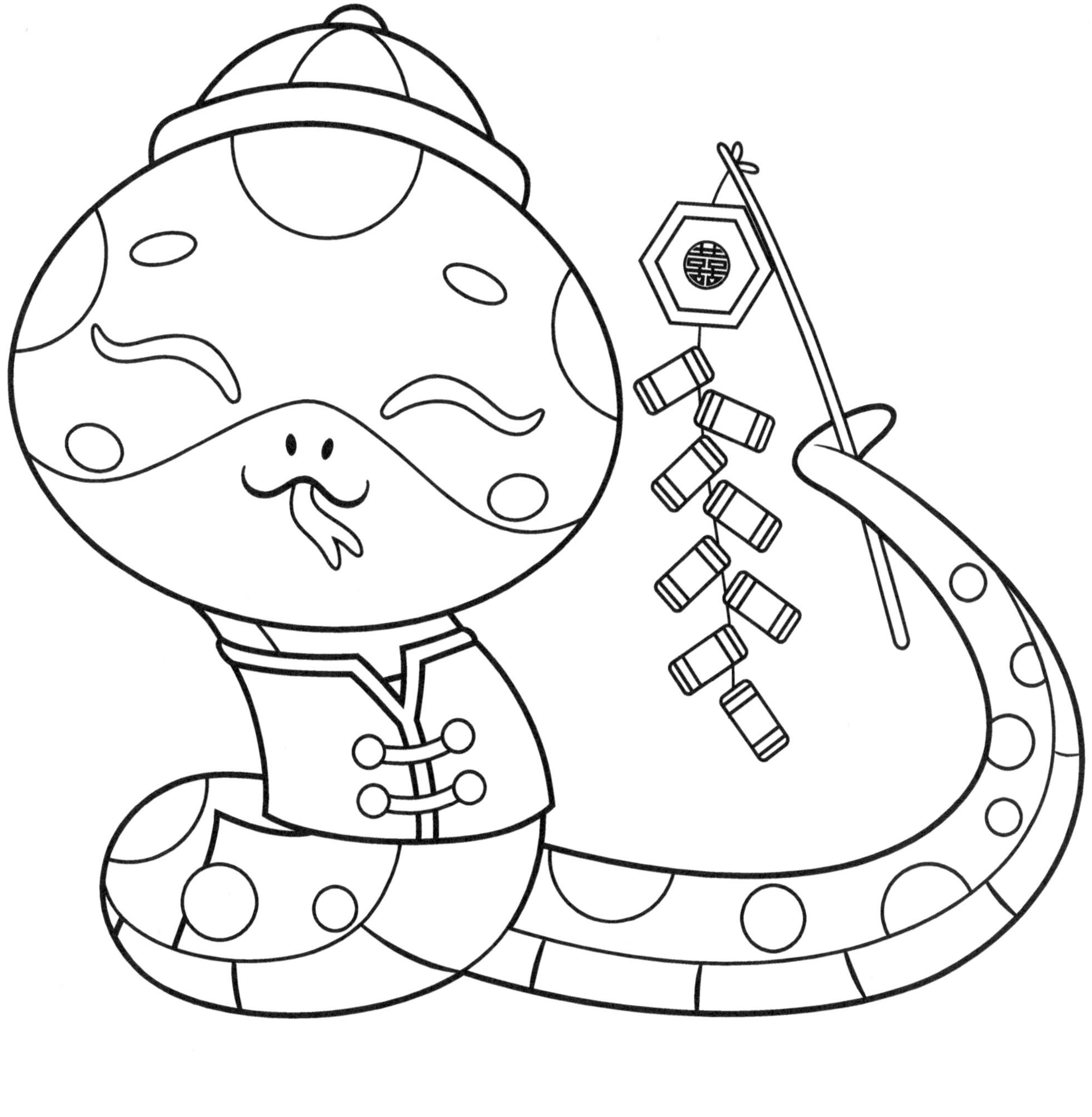

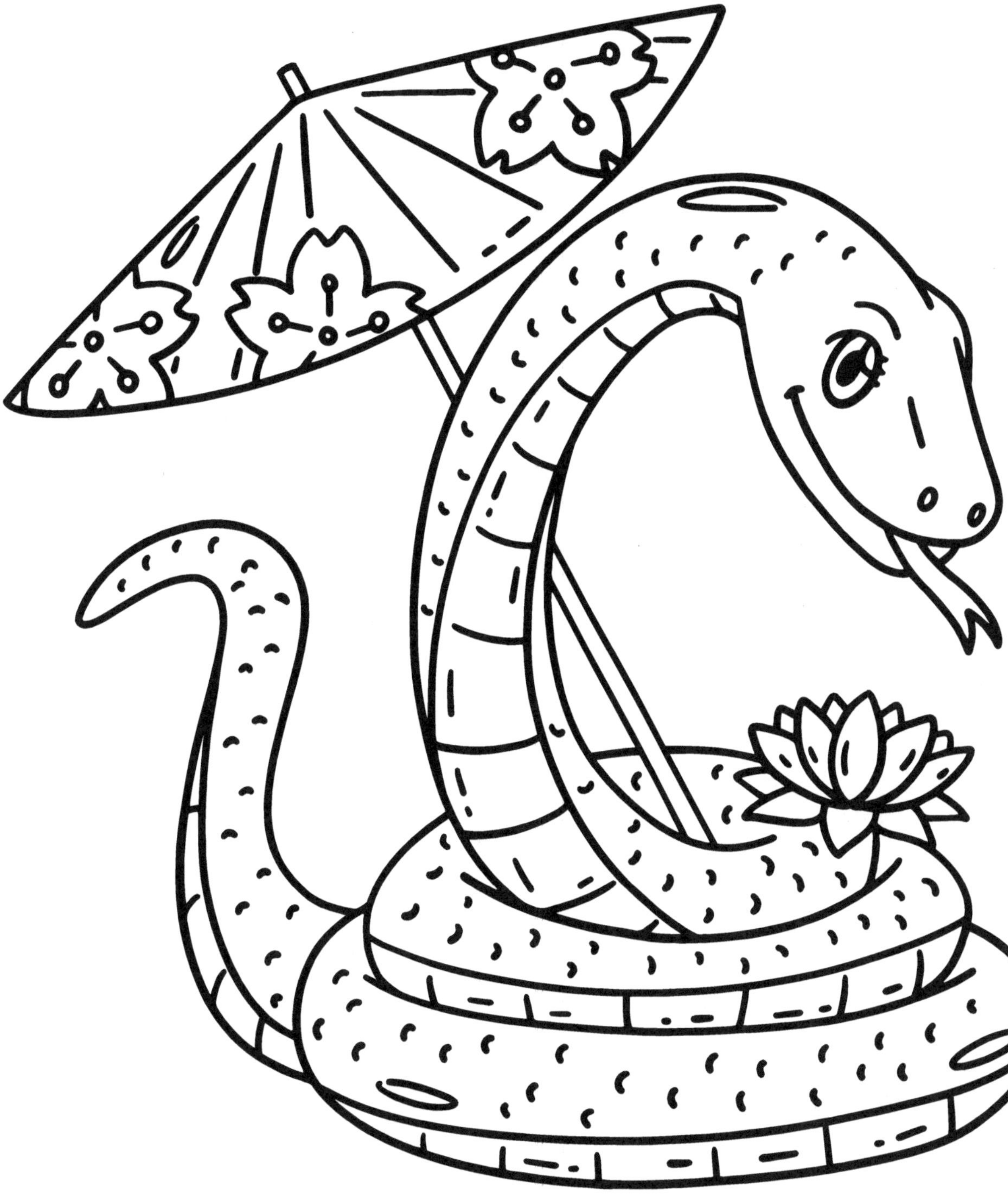

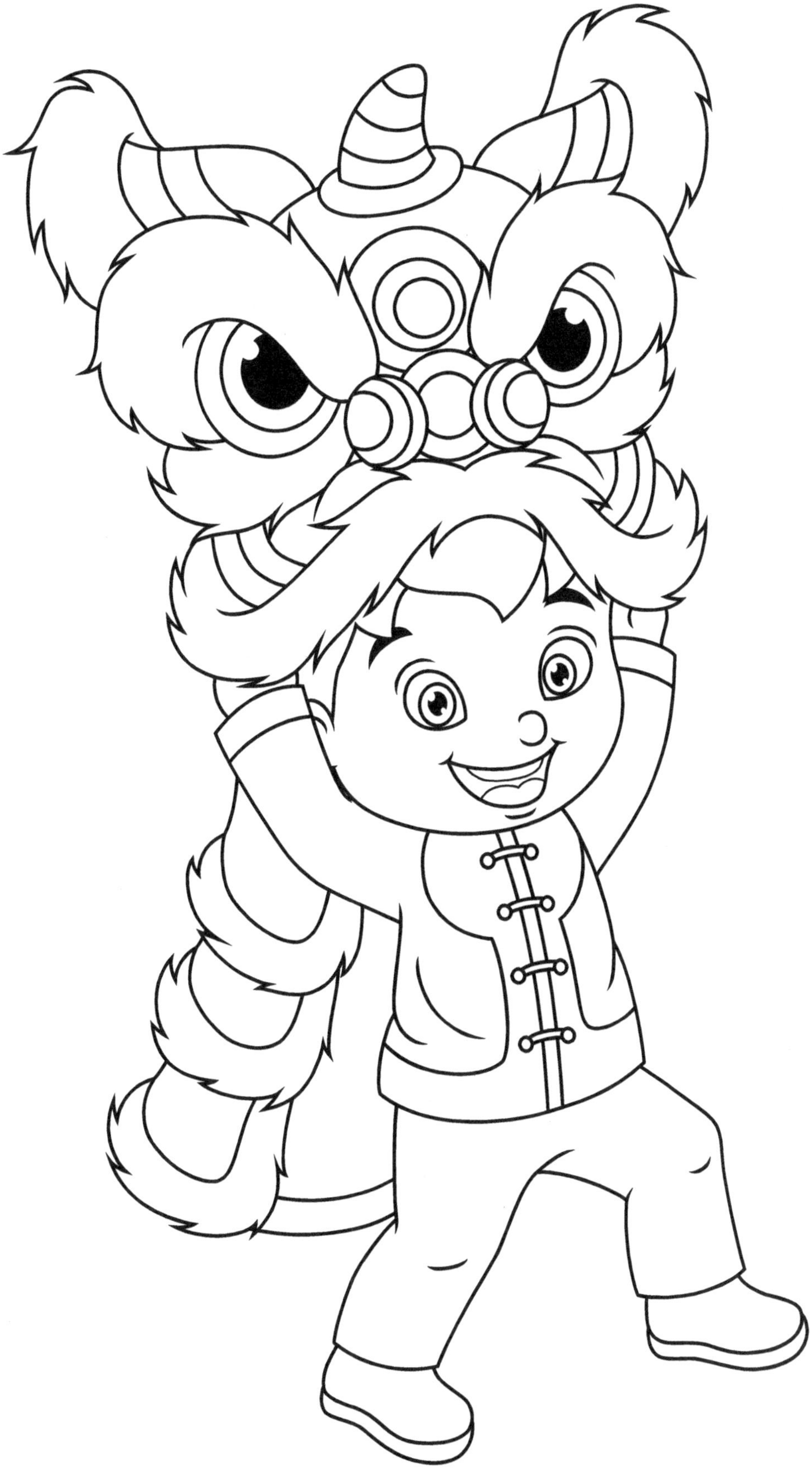

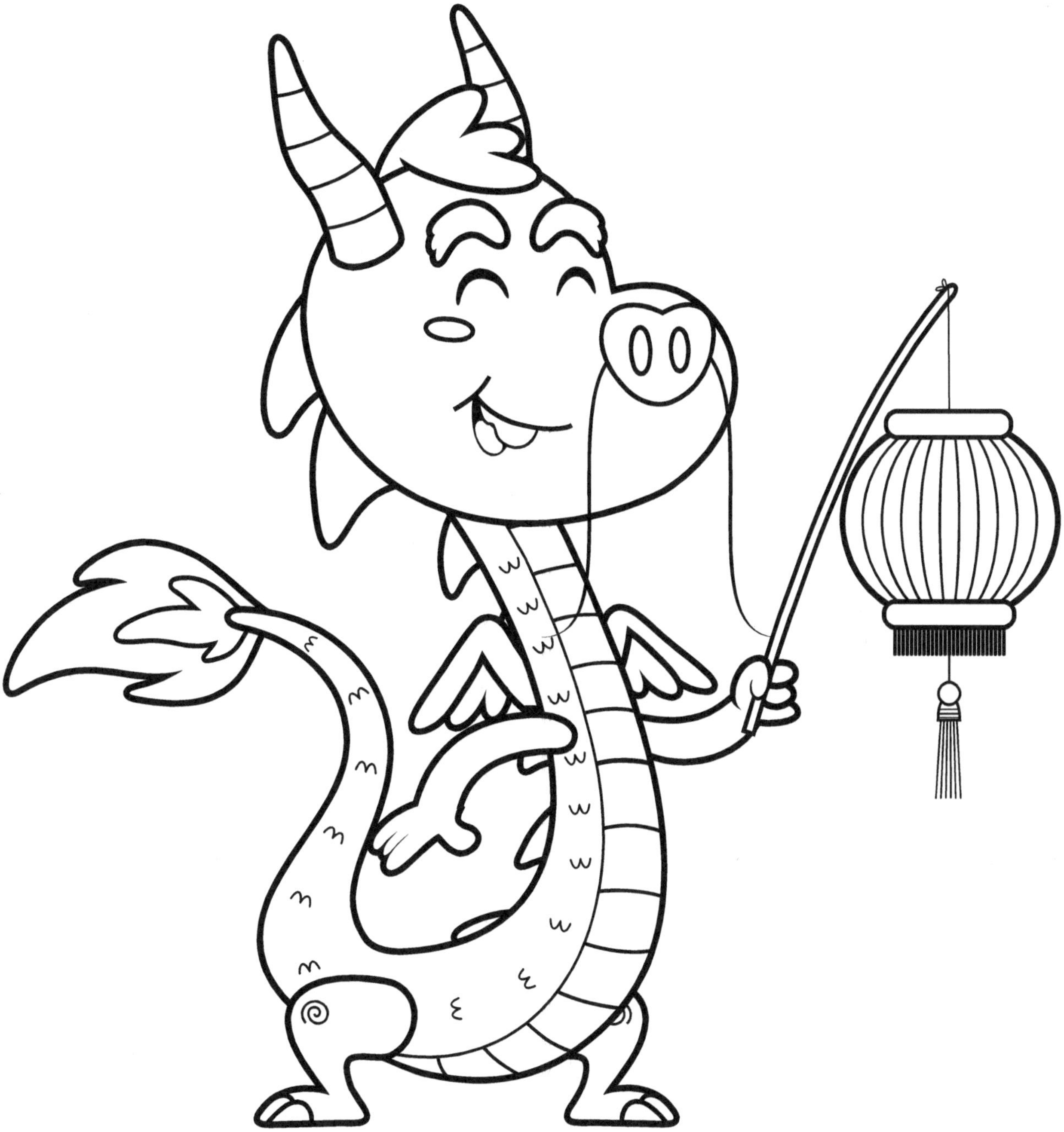

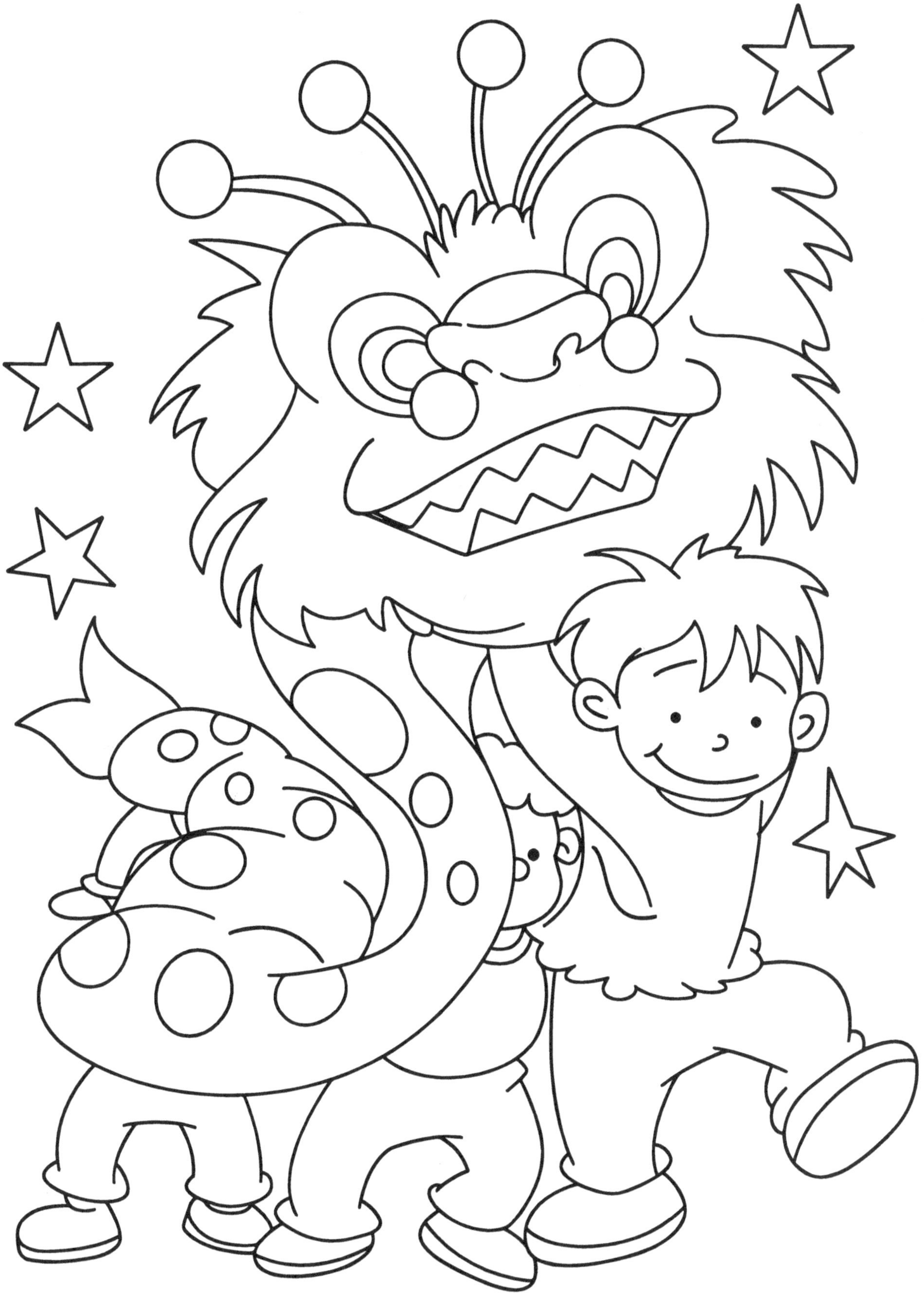

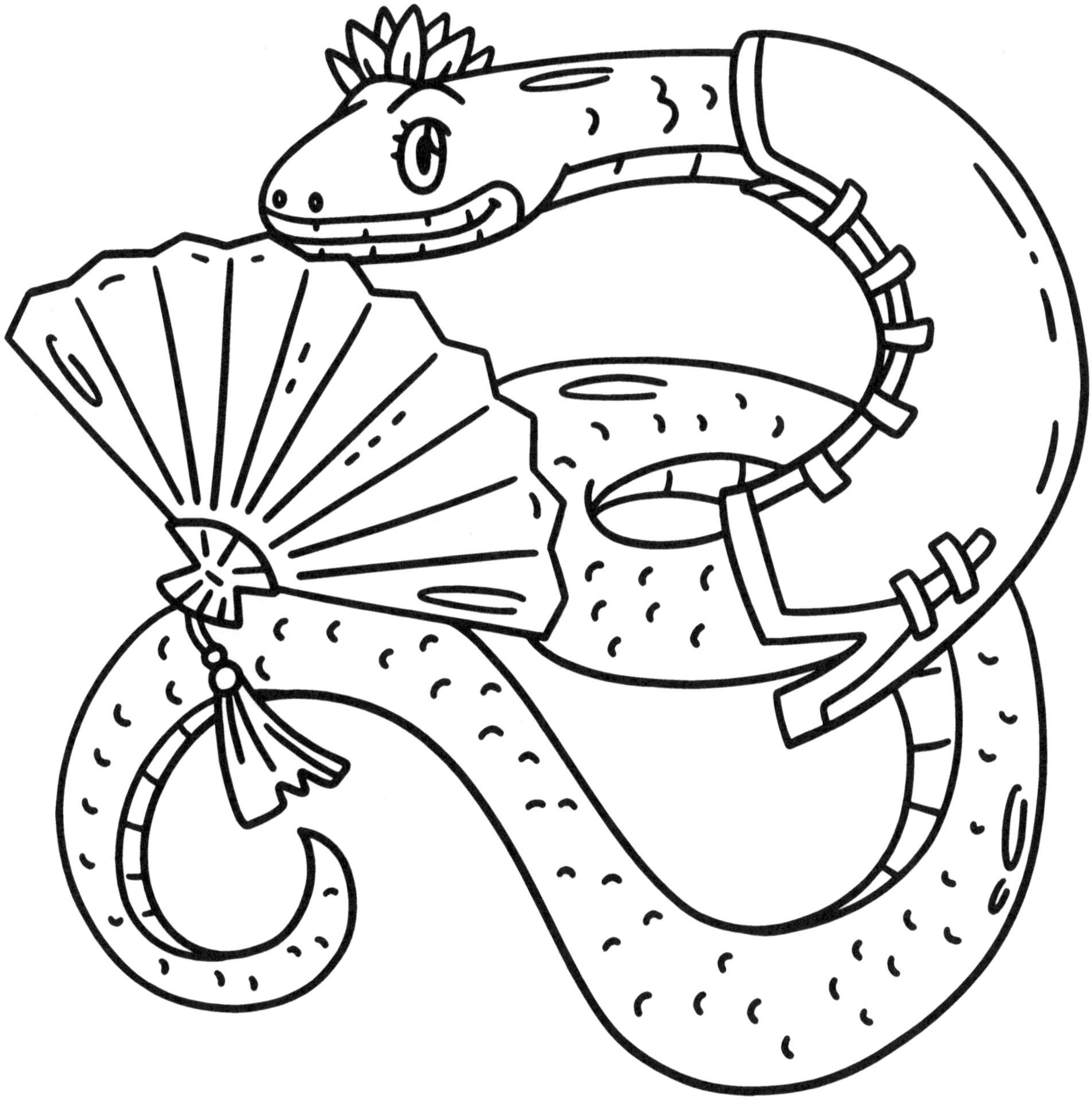

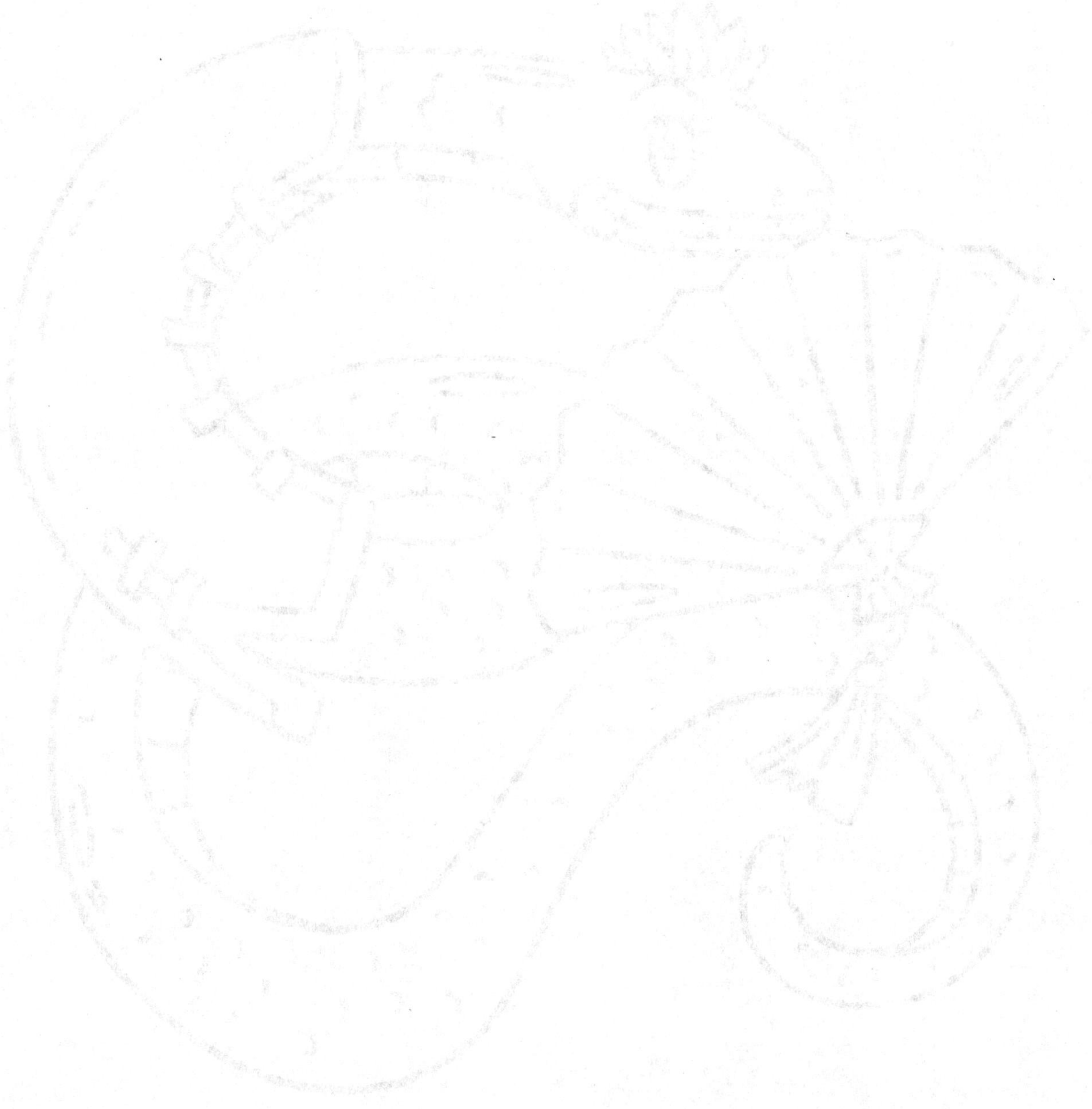

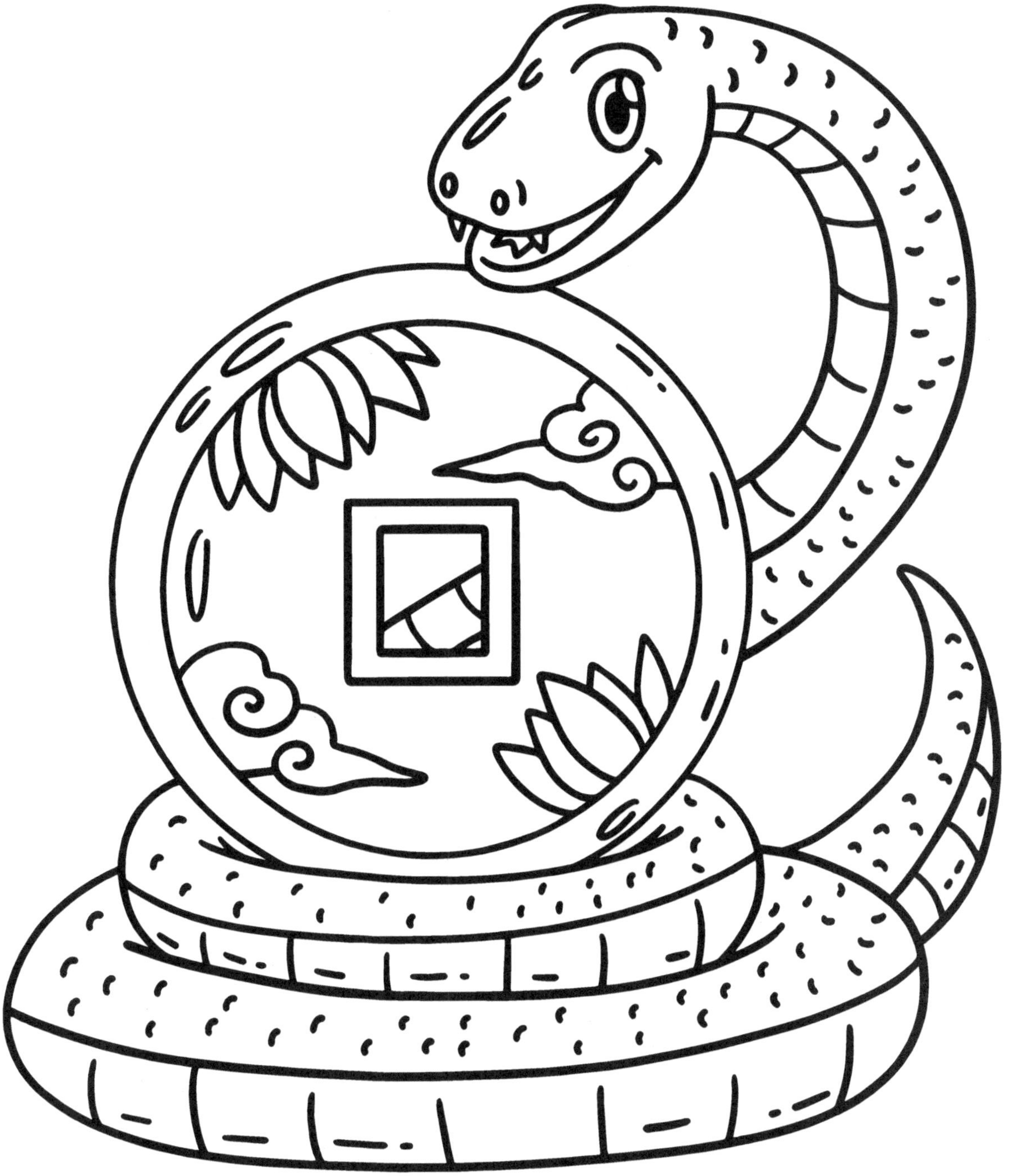

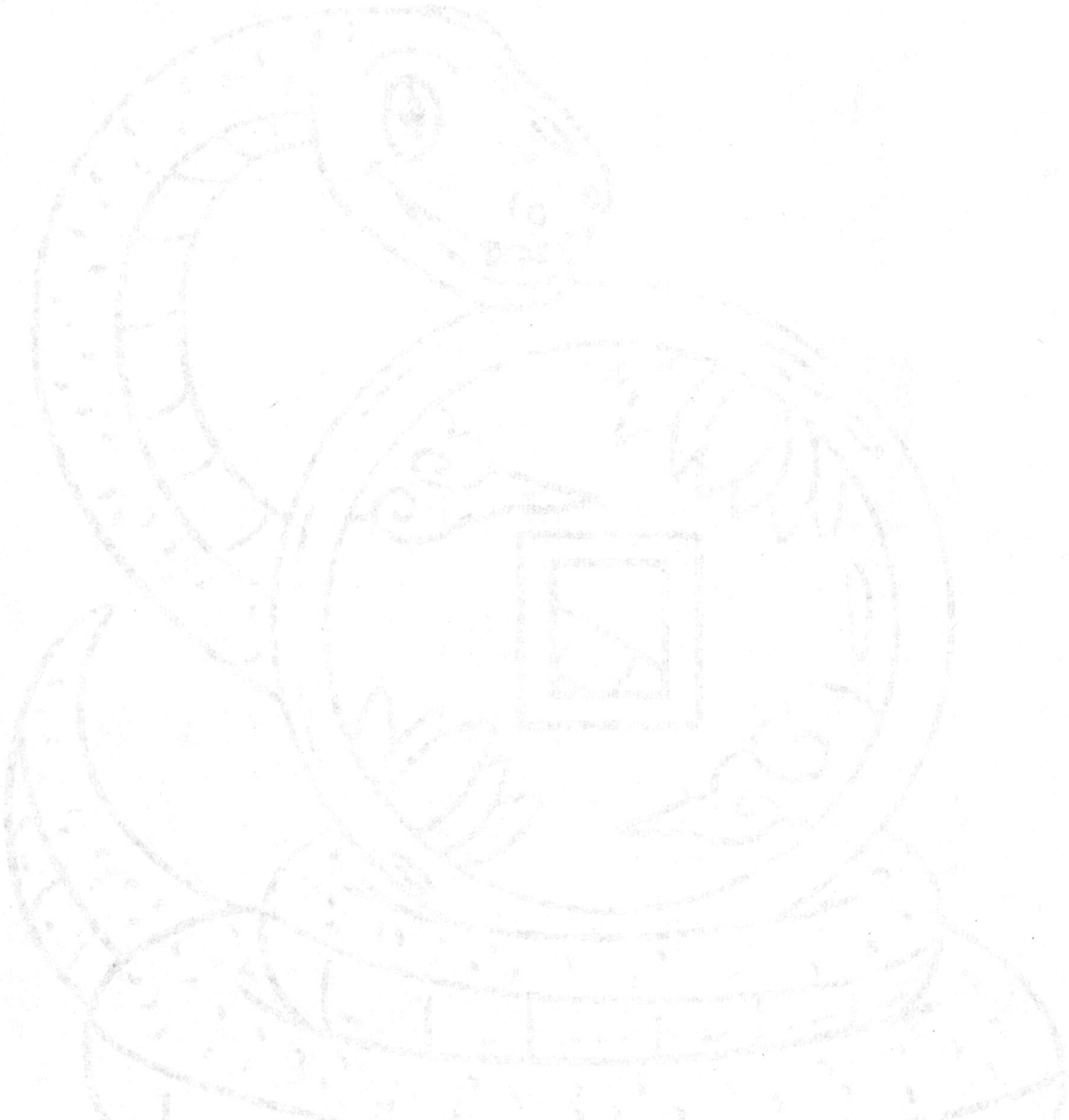

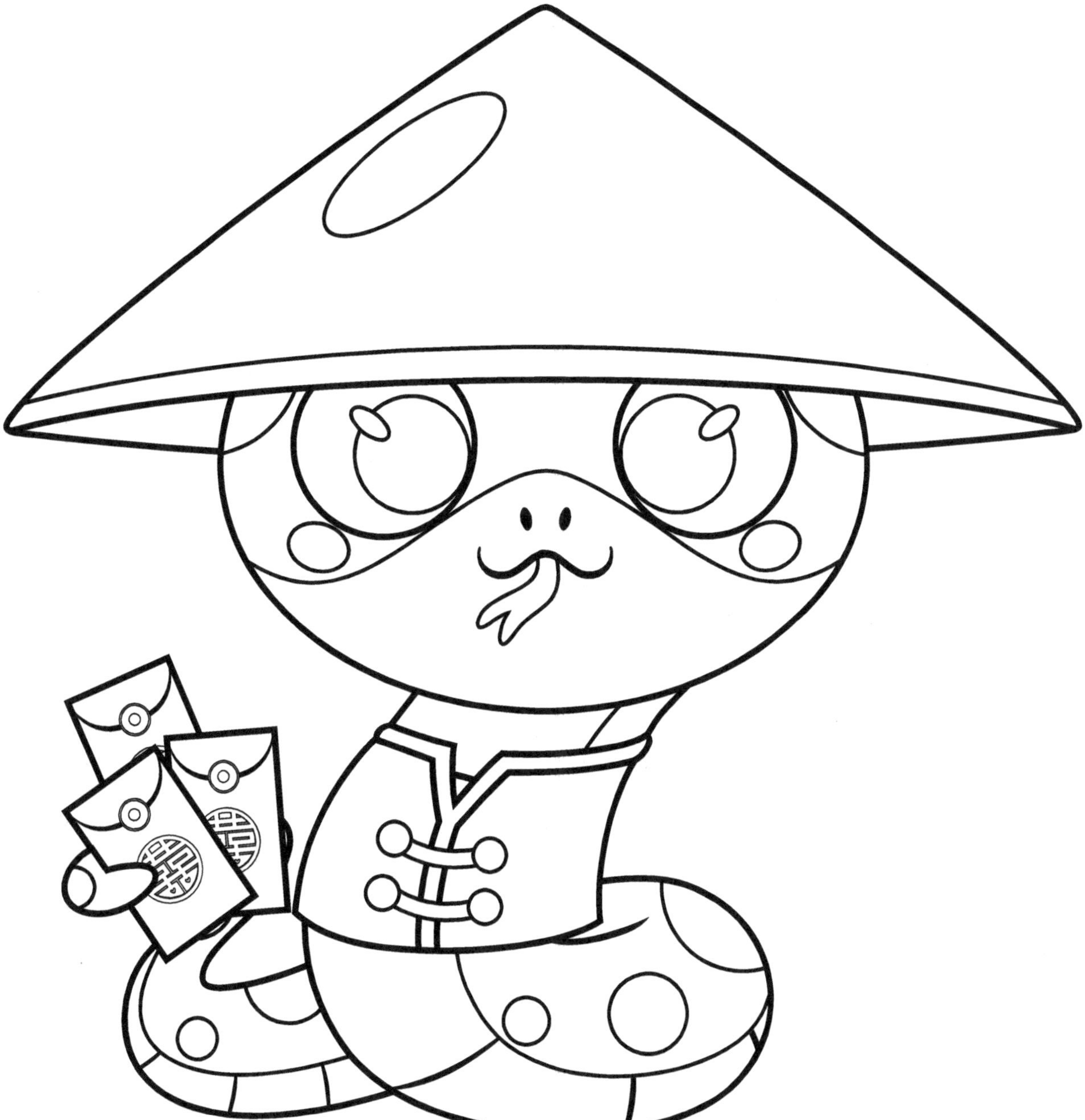

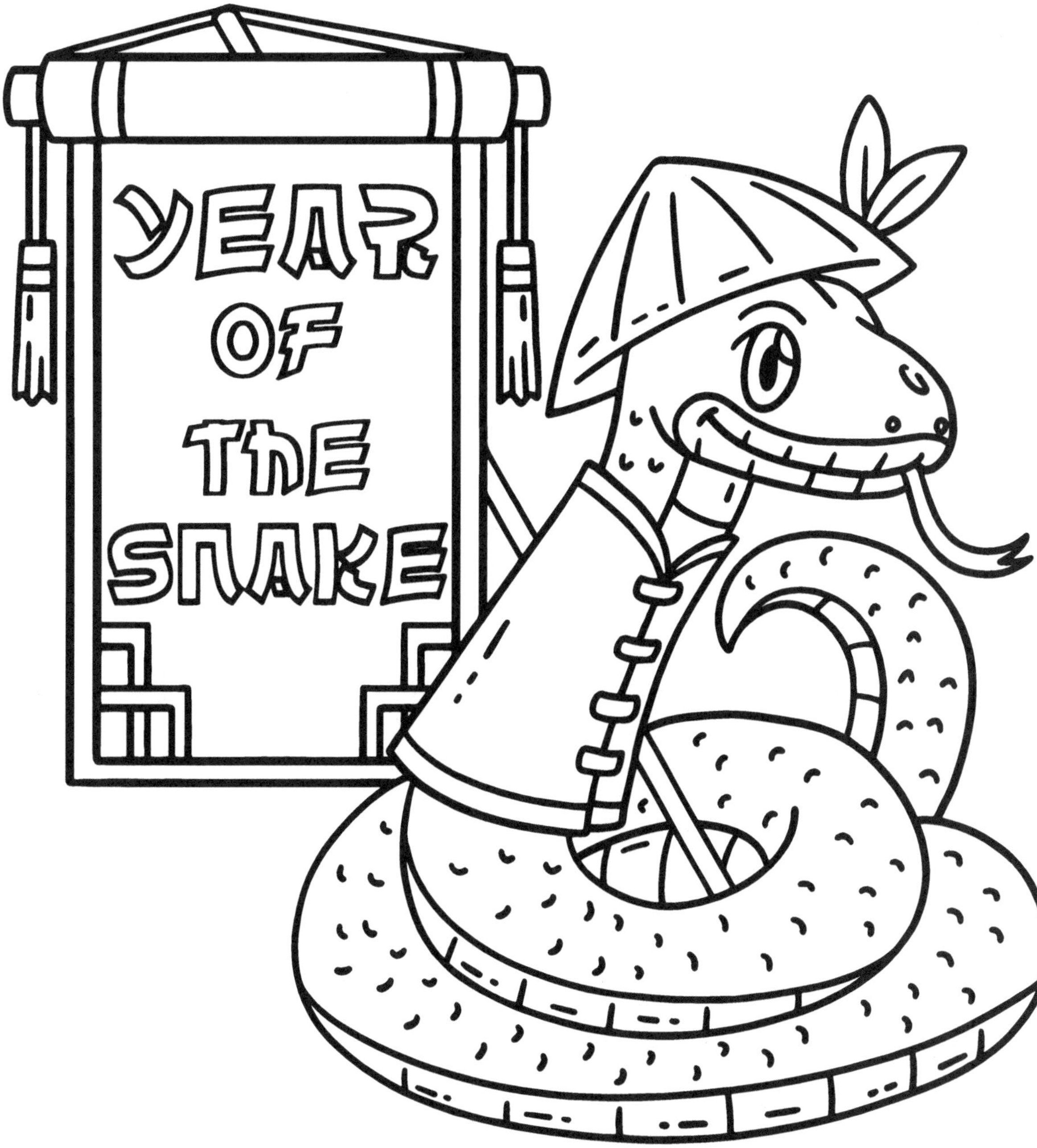
YEAR OF THE SNAKE

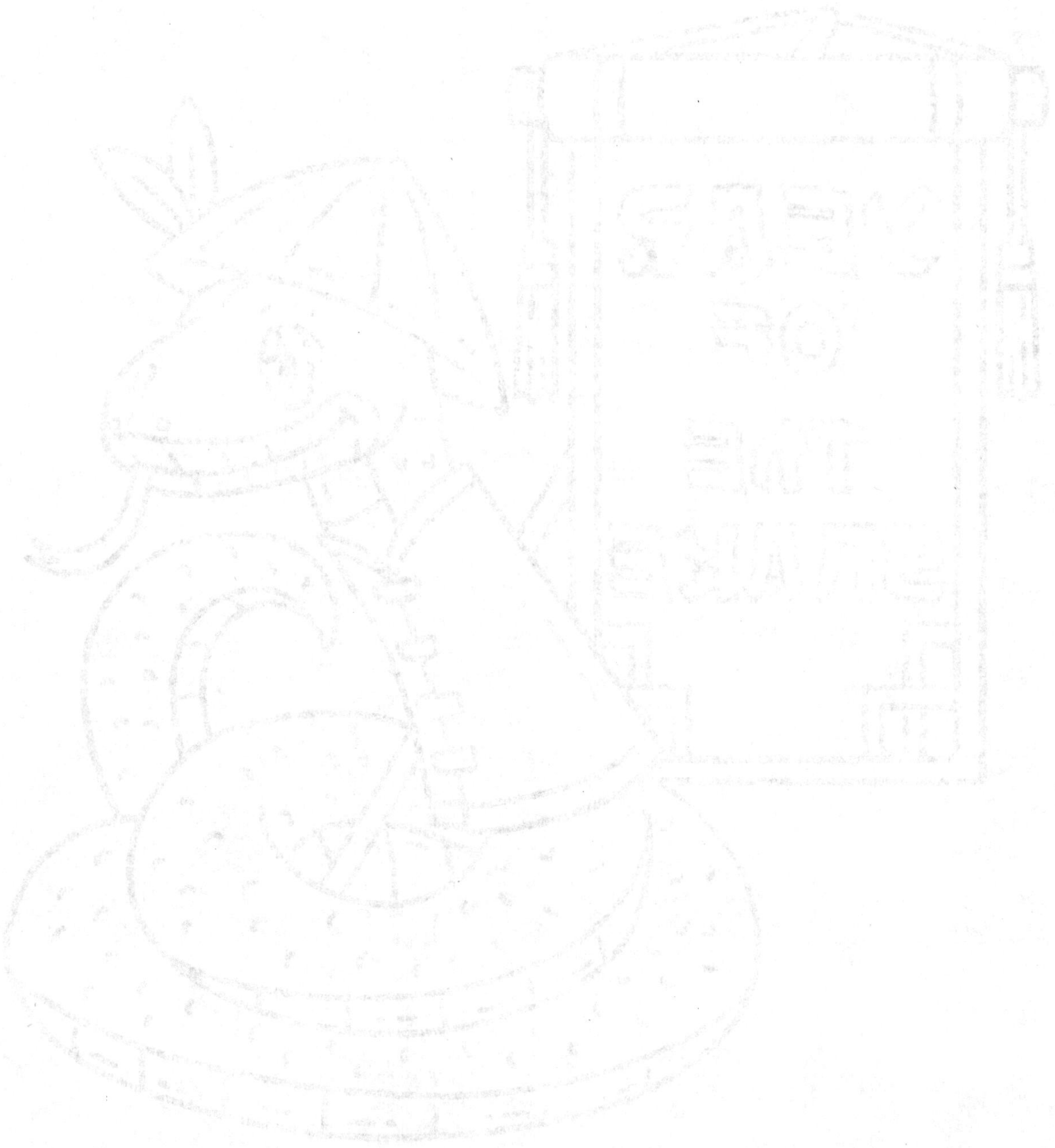

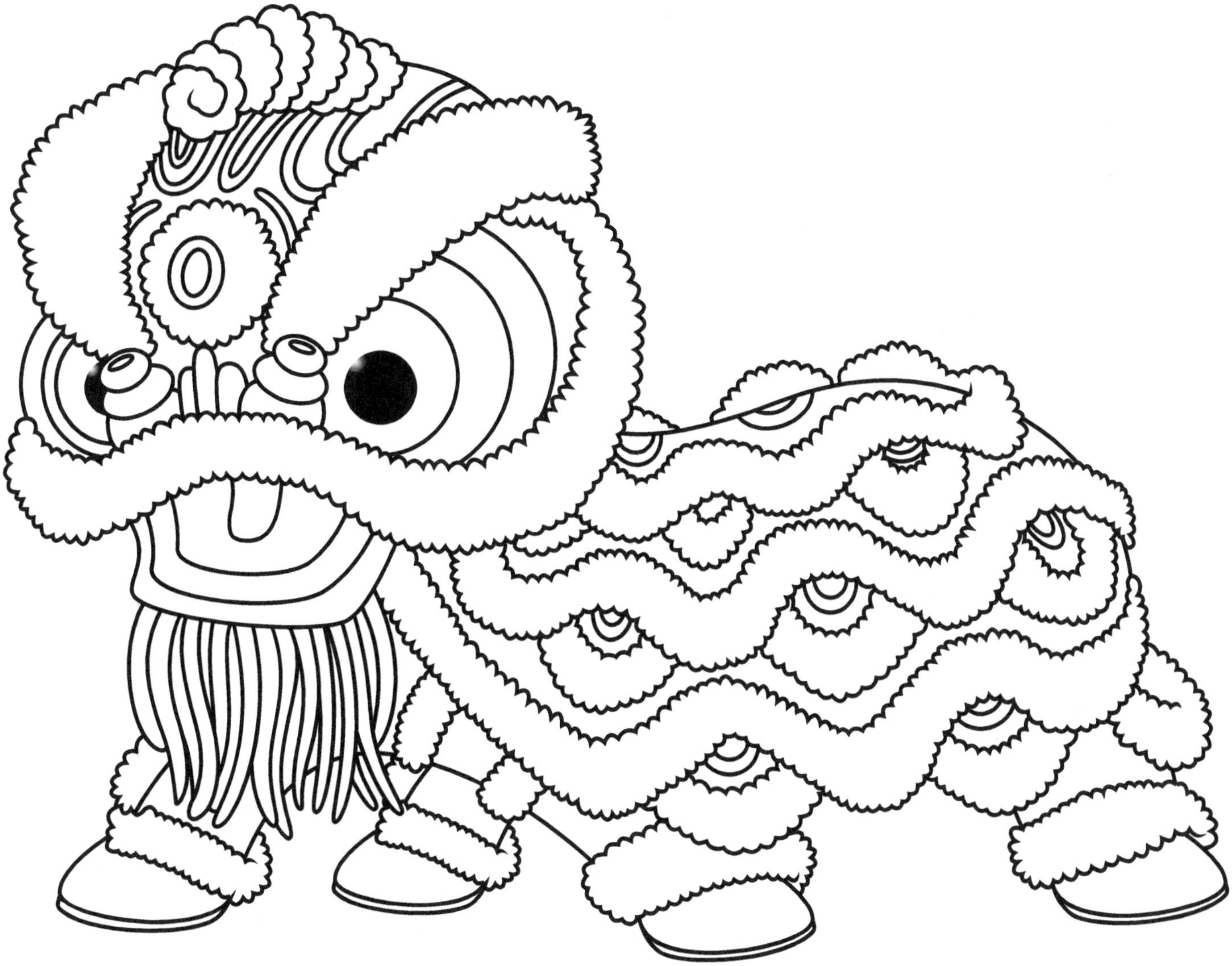

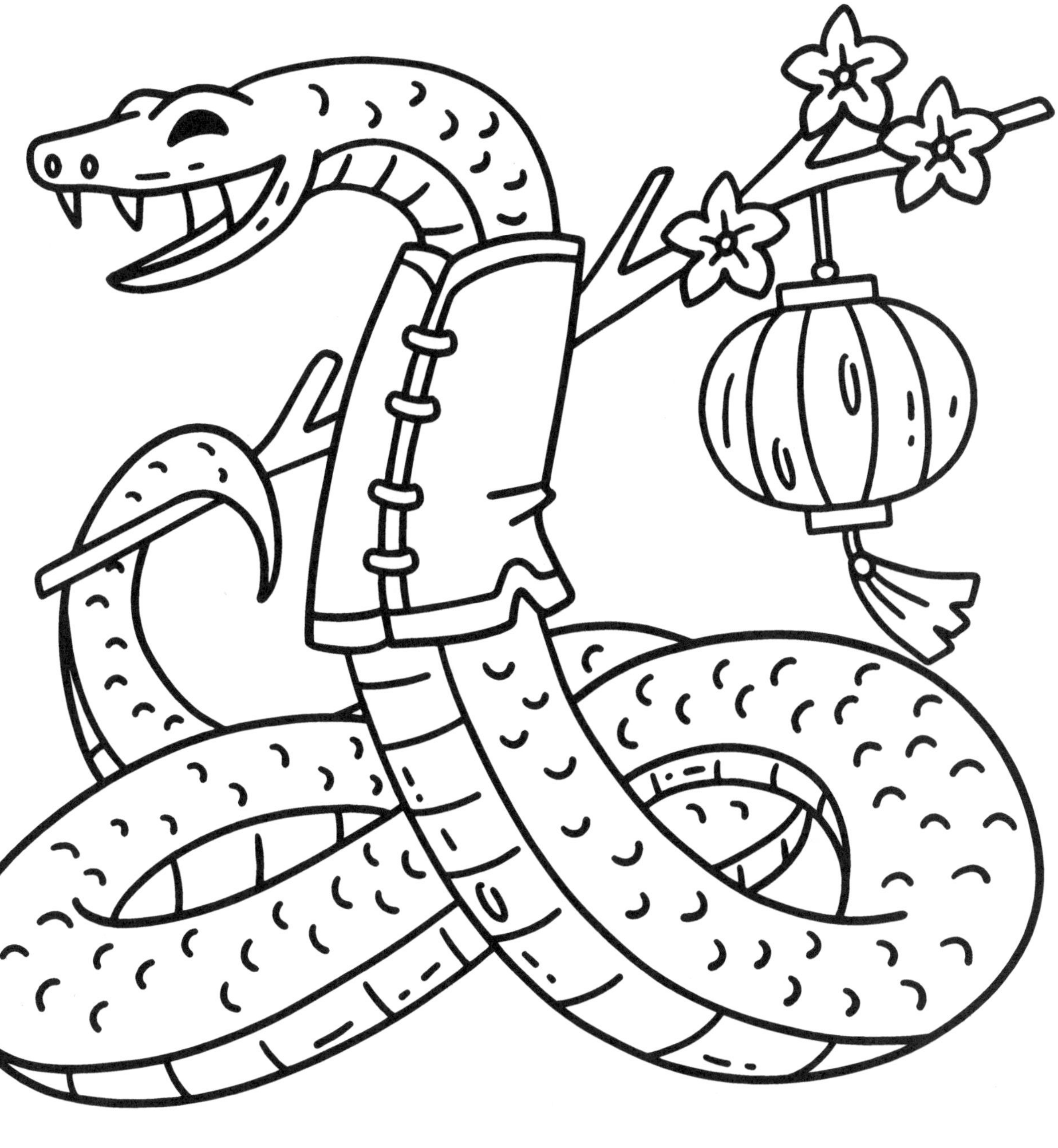

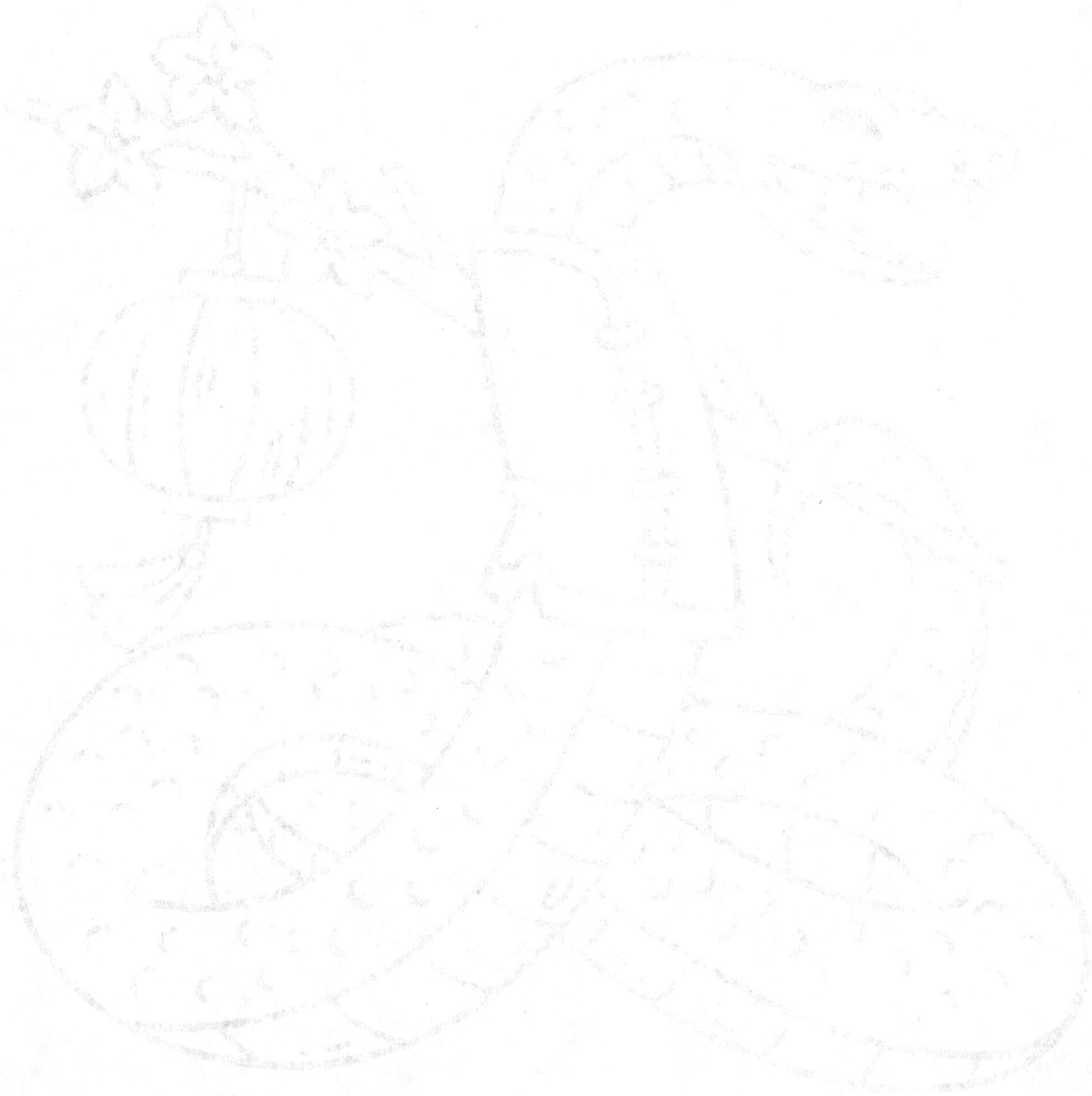

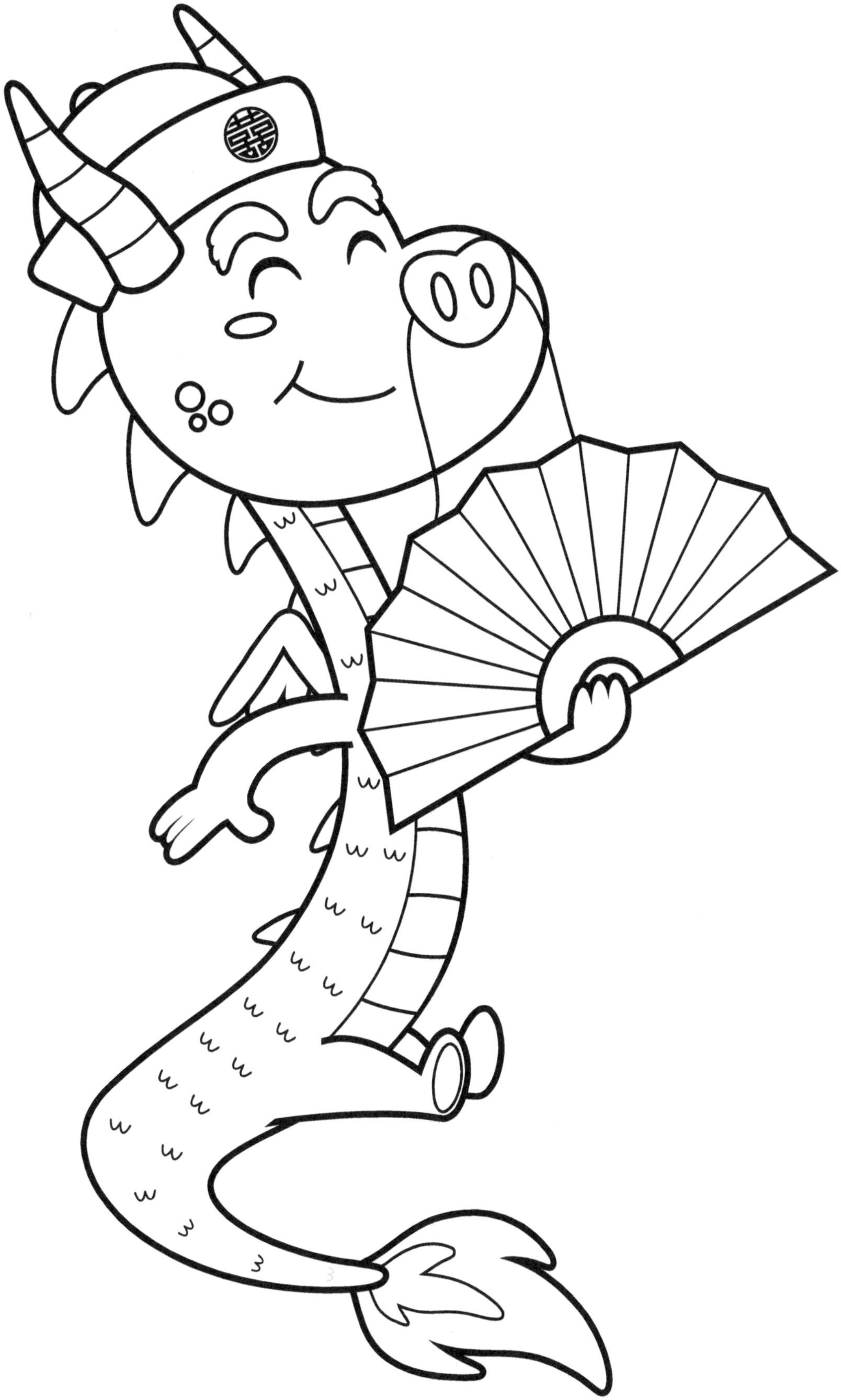

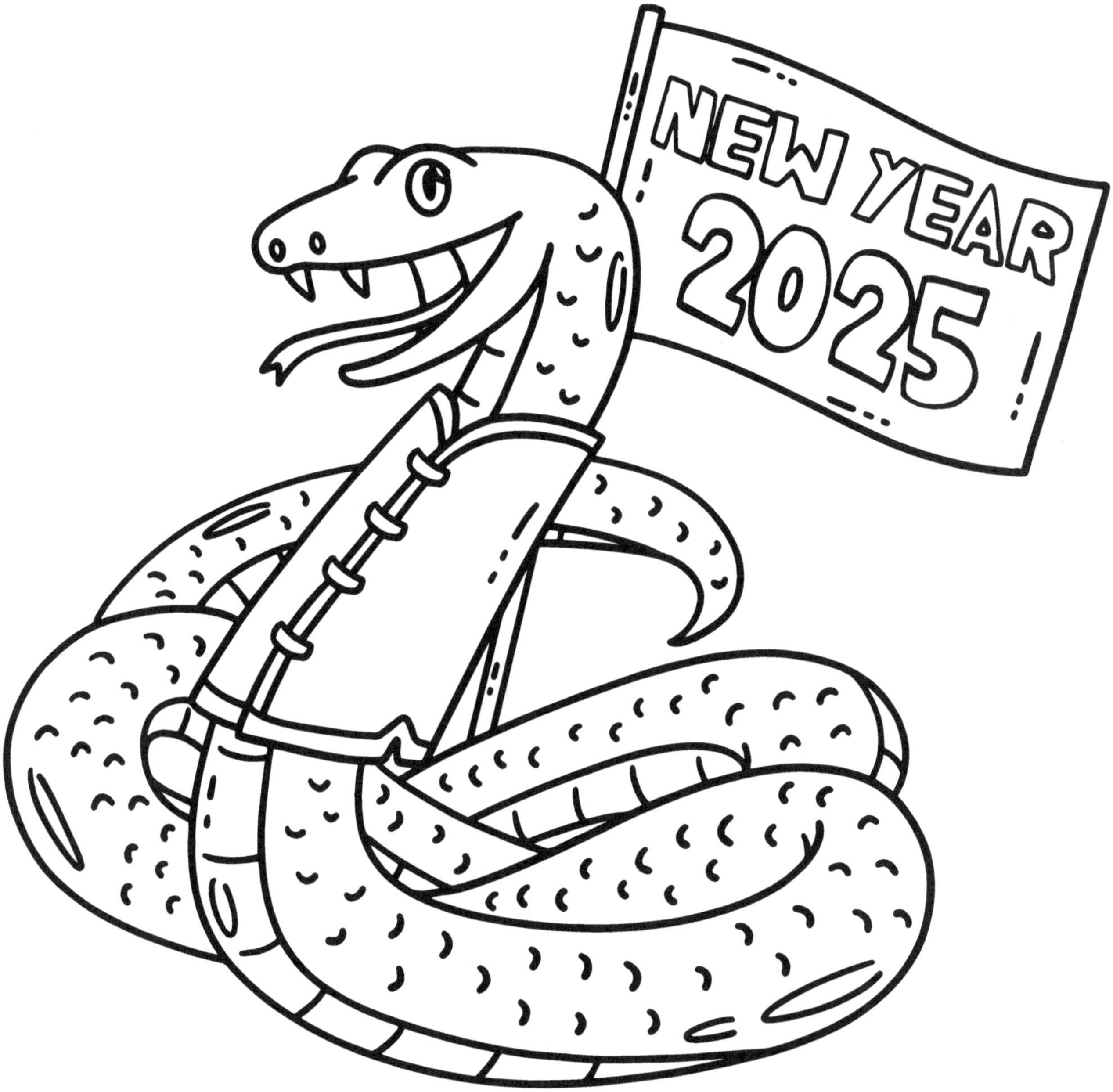
NEW YEAR
2025

Made in United States
Troutdale, OR
01/08/2025

27727869R00031